GEEZER STORIES

GEEZER STORIES

THE CARE & FEEDING
OF
OLD PEOPLE

LAURA MANSFIELD

WordCrafts

For my parents.

Chapter 1

Forget The Past. Let It Go.

"I know all about conditional love. I was raised on it."

–DooDaddy

My earliest memory of my mother is of her walking beside the pool, backlit by the bright morning sun, like a goddess. Her heels clicked on the pavement. Her hair shone in the light. Her tiny waist was cinched in above a full skirt, all Betty Draper-style. She glowed. And I was proud that she was my mine. Then she was gone. I was having a swimming lesson with my sister in the frigid unheated pool at Cherokee Country Club. My mother was playing bridge in the River Room above. Eating triangle-shaped club sandwiches with the crusts cut off and those little toothpicks wearing cellophane party hats.

We often visited my grandmother in Knoxville, Tennessee for the summer. Keeling, my sister, and I would be dropped off for a month to attend Webb School Day Camp and take swimming lessons at

Cherokee and to give my mother a break from the burden of parenting three small children under the age of four. Dad was always working, working, working. Mom was busy playing bridge and tennis and Junior League-ing. We moved around a lot because of Dad's job, six houses in five different towns before I was in second grade. In each new neighborhood, we kids entertained ourselves. Back in those days, there were no electronic devices, and there was very little supervision. Yes, there were chicken potpies (pronounced chicken pock pies) and a series of inattentive teenage babysitters, but mostly we ran wild.

I remember living briefly in Springfield, Tennessee where my best friend was a little punk-faced girl named Tricinda Broyles. Her mother was a hairdresser, so Tricinda was usually home alone. We reveled in our independence and defiance. Cindy and I scampered around shoeless and shirtless, climbing trees and pretending we were boys—until my brother tattled. We had our own street gang of tricycle-riding toddlers, including my brother and his Big Wheel. We rode our bikes barefoot and dragged our feet to stop. Watched "The Twilight Zone" after school and freaked ourselves out. Ate Wonder Bread rolled up in dough balls. Then we threw darts at the bull's eye target in Tricinda's garage until we got bored and threw them at each other. I walked home with a metal dart sticking out of the side of my head. And I didn't even cry.

So now when I look into my mother's ancient face, and see her pale blue eyes, blue as the summer sky behind her that day at the pool, I have very little recognition of her as my mother. She is more of a vaguely familiar relative, someone who's always been around in the background, but we have no real connection. No memories of her brushing my hair or reading to me or helping me with my homework, much less playing with me. I never told her about my crushes. We never discussed boys and fashion when I was a teenager. I didn't tell her when I got my period. She didn't come to the hospital when I gave birth to my only son. And yet, she is my mother. And I feel the obligation to be a good daughter. The daughter she always wanted. And maybe, just maybe, if I'm good enough, she'll magically transform into the mother I never had.

When Mom had her stroke, or whatever it was last winter, it set off a chain reaction of events that landed my parents on twin walkers in a retirement community, both greatly diminished versions of themselves. And I found myself in the clichéd role of my generation —the Taffy Generation—caring for my elderly parents, while still caring for my own family, in my case, a recently acquired 10-year-old stepson, who alit in my newly empty nest, like a changeling, a fragile little bird, completely different from the confident, independent, self-sufficient eaglet that had just taken flight.

Those early days in the hospital after my mother's episode, I slept in the uncomfortable chair beside her bed, never thinking to ask how it folded out into a cot. I was new to this now all-too-familiar world of ambulances, ERs and scrubs-clad therapists, nurses, assistants, technicians, nutritionists, counselors, and other manner of caregivers and administrators that see to The Care and Feeding of Old People. I bathed my mother and helped her to and from the potty-chair, tubes attached and beepers blaring. I brushed her hair and put lotion on her tissue-paper skin. And I sat. I kept a bedside vigil, watching over her, protecting her from the unknown, from the future, from pain and suffering, from the bogeyman.

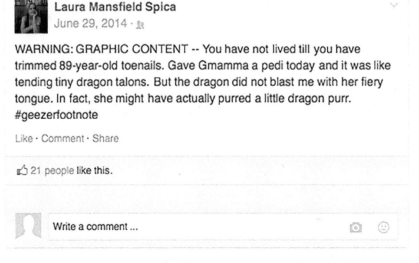

Laura Mansfield Spica
June 29, 2014 ·

WARNING: GRAPHIC CONTENT -- You have not lived till you have trimmed 89-year-old toenails. Gave Gmamma a pedi today and it was like tending tiny dragon talons. But the dragon did not blast me with her fiery tongue. In fact, she might have actually purred a little dragon purr. #geezerfootnote

Like · Comment · Share

21 people like this.

Write a comment …

My younger brother and older sister live out of town. They come when they can. But mostly it's me. The Middle Child. The Good

Daughter. The Dutiful One. Shuttling my parents to and from doctors' appointments and funerals, delivering Depends and Metamucil on demand. Sitting in their stifling hot apartment (geezers are cold-natured and jack the heat way up) helping them work the crossword puzzle. And still I remember watching them dance at my debutante balls. Seeing them leaving for football games and cocktail parties, my mother dripping in pearls, swathed in fur and smelling of Chanel No. 5.

We've found a way to stay connected, despite our lack of a shared past, my parents and I. And we try to see the humor in the situation. I've grown very fond of these old people, who are now my parents, who are nothing like they were when I was growing up. They've mellowed into caricatures of their former selves.

Laura Mansfield Spica
November 6, 2014 ·

GEEZER UPDATE: It's crossword puzzle time, a breakfast tradition as old as dirt. Every morning, DooDaddy makes a "Xerox Copy" of the crossword and gives Gmamma the original, which she works in pen, just to intimidate him.
DooDaddy: "15 across ... hmmm ... Viking Base ... N-O-E-W blank blank."
Gmamma: "It's N-O-R-W where Vikings come from." (insert eye roll)
DooDaddy: "Where Vikings come from ... hmmm ... the North? Norseland?
Gmamma: "NORWAY!!!"
DooDaddy: "Branched horn, six letters ... boy, these are hard."
Me: "Think Rudolph the Red-Nosed Reindeer." (doing finger antlers on my head)
Gmamma begins laughing until her eyes water.
DooDaddy laughs too and wheezes himself into a coughing fit.
We all forget why we're laughing ...
Me, remembering: "What does Rudolph have on his head?"
DooDaddy: "Branched horns?"

Like · Comment · Share

 37 people like this.

 Write a comment ...

Dad, aka DooDaddy, as he's known to my son and now to the world, was a mercurial, charming, brilliant man in his prime. He chain-smoked and worked constantly (retail is a demanding mistress), with little energy or desire left over for hands-on parenting. As children, we lived for any brief encounter with him, both in fear and in awe of this wondrous, mysterious man, our father. Just to hear his heavy, confident steps as we cowered under the dining room table, shrouded with Indian blankets, was both thrilling and frightening. Mom made heavy use of the wait-til-your-father-gets-home threat, as she chased us around the house with a fly swatter or a "switch" crafted from a sapling branch. We were sent to select our own switches to heighten the drama and dread.

 Laura Mansfield Spica
April 21, 2015 ·

GEEZER UPDATE: In which DooDaddy opines on art, genealogy and war
Me: "Now who painted that landscape again? Your grandfather?"
DooDaddy: "No, it was my great grandfather, Louis Bryson Wiley, who graduated from Erskine College in Due West, South Carolina. He was an artist and a photographer and almost a preacher."
Me: "And he was Mammie Jo's first husband?"
DooDaddy: "Yes, he married my great-grandmother, Josephine Scott, Mammie Jo. But he was the least bit consumtive ..."
Me: "Does that mean he had tuberculosis?"
DooDaddy: "Yes, so he died. Then Mammie Jo married Mr. Lauderdale, because she was the prettiest young widow in Fayetteville."
Me: "So there were a lot of young widows in Fayetteville?"
DooDaddy: "Yes, because it was the Civil War, and all the young men of Fayetteville, well really all of Lincoln County, joined the Tennessee Infantry to fight in the Battle of Cheat Mountain in Northwest Virginia, and barely any of them returned."
Me: "That's so sad."
DooDaddy: "It was a disastrous escapade."

Like · Comment · Share

 41 people like this.

 Write a comment ...

Later on we talked politics and books and business with our father. Dad was up on everything, had a point of view but could play the devil's advocate just to make us think about both sides of an issue. It was intellectually thrilling. He could expound on any topic and explain any complex concept. He was made to parent grown children, more than little ones.

In fact, my parents would readily admit to not liking children, except for their own, of course. Truth be told, they didn't really like us either. But they loved us, and they did the best they could. My dad was an orphan raised on conditional love by his grandparents and his five Southern belle aunts like something out of a Truman Capote story. He never learned how to parent, because he never had parents of his own.

My mother was the spoiled, sheltered daughter of her own doting mother. Her third-generation physician father died early; her brother joined the army, and she and my grandmother led a privileged life in a gilded world that prepared my mother for "society" but not for reality. She and Grandmother had lots of "help," including a cook who prepared most of their meals. Mom could dance, paint, speak French and make beef stroganoff & spinach soufflé (her signature meal when she and Dad were dating). She had done the requisite European tour and written a thesis on Wordsworth. She was well educated and well read. She worked briefly in advertising, living on cigarettes, coffee and pecan pie, before marrying my father.

Don't get me wrong. This is no "Mommy Dearest" memoir. Hell, nothing makes you appreciate your parents and forgive them their shortcomings like being a parent yourself.

You. Do. The. Best. You. Can. Period.

Rule #1 for The Care and Feeding of Old People: Forget the past. Let it go.

It was a different era, the one we grew up in. We rode bikes *without helmets*, for goodness sake. We disappeared barefoot into the neighborhood till dark, and even after, running across the wet grass, catching lightening bugs in glass jars. Yes, we ran *with glass jars* in our hands. Maybe even scissors. We played Spin-The-Bottle in our friends' basements and in the parking lot of the Ice Chalet. Parents were simply less attentive then. So when I found out in my thirties that my own brother had been sexually abused by a neighbor from the time he was five until he was seven years old, I was devastated. Why didn't I save him? Why didn't I protect him? Where was I when this was going on? And where were our parents?

Flash forward to now, when I know exactly where they are, dozing in their chairs like contented cats. Fully dressed. Just waiting for something to happen. Gmamma, as she's known to my son and now to the world, was an avid reader, always had a stack of library books at the ready, reading in the pick-up line as she chauffeured us to and from school and myriad after-school activities—art lessons and horseback riding for me, ballet and Girl Scouts for my sister (I never made it past Brownies), piano for everyone, because that's just what you did, right? And tennis lessons for my brother. We were never at a loss for extracurricular activities. Raised to be well-rounded renaissance children, cultured and exposed to the arts, with the thought that we would find our passion and follow it.

Later we segued into activities of our own choosing, track, cross-country and swimming for me. I had been "frail" as a child, painfully thin. Mom told me she had always wanted to be frail (weird, right?), so that was enough to motivate me to drink body-building milkshakes that tasted like sand and train like a maniac, running by myself up and down our dead-end street, powering out hundreds of sit-ups, calf-raises and push-ups. I was *not* going to be frail. Or a victim. Or need anyone's help. Ever. Because there had never been anyone to help me in the first place. You can't miss what you never had. When I awoke from nightmares as a child, I lay panting in my bed, my heart thumping out of my chest, paralyzed by fear. It never occurred to me to call out for my mother. That simply wasn't an option. Stiff upper lip. Stoicism. Suck it up. That was the ticket.

I do remember staying home sick from school at one point and being brought scrambled egg sandwiches by—wait for it—the "maid." Yup, that's what we called housekeepers back then. Mom must have had a bridge game or a tennis match or been volunteering as a Pink Lady at the hospital. Did I mention the bowling league at the country club? Stay-at-home moms didn't actually stay at home. They did "good works" and socialized with other stay-at-home-moms. So I languished in bed and savored the warm gummy feel of the white bread against the hot salty eggs in my mouth. Bless that woman, whose name I can't remember now. Annie, maybe? She was one of a series of housekeepers we had in those days. There was no real continuity. But she made me feel cared for. And attended to. Briefly.

Laura Mansfield Spica
November 21, 2014 ·

GEEZER BONUS: I painted Gmamma's tiny toe talons pearlescent pink and she was giddy with delight ... like the little girl I never had.

Like · Comment · Share

👍 28 people like this.

Write a comment ...

~

There have been surrogate mothers, to be sure. In fact, I think I put up with my narcissistic high-school boyfriend simply because I had a crush on his mom. Well, that's not entirely true. I loved him madly, truly, deeply in the way only a sixteen-year-old girl can love (#puppylove). And he ignored me, took me for granted, cheated on me, and carved his initials in my back with a pocketknife. But his mom was an angel.

Insert sidebar here that a distant, emotionally unavailable boyfriend who could melt my girlish heart with his chocolate eyes and then cut me off at the knees with a cruel remark was the perfect manifestation of my parents.

Kelly was the yin and yang, the charisma and the coldness I was weaned on. A poor but inevitable choice.

I'll never forget going to his house for dinner—Friday night was steak night—did I mention his dad was awesome too? Anyhow, Mr. Clevenger would grill filets out back (we didn't cook outside at home, didn't own a grill) and Mrs. Clevenger would serve sun tea, brewed up in a big old glass pitcher with lots of sugar added. There may have even been fresh mint from their backyard garden involved. Then we'd all gather around the kitchen table, Jan, my boyfriend's sister, and Kelly, my neglectful, sarcastic and (to me) irresistible boyfriend and his parents for a "family dinner."

There would be broccoli casserole made by Jan, cooking along-side her mother, after cutting out a dress pattern on the den floor together. I was mesmerized by this mother/daughter interaction. The Clevengers rode bikes and grilled steaks and prayed together. They grew corn and tomatoes right there in the backyard of their suburban home together. Anything seemed possible with that level of togetherness.

Mrs. Clevenger was so sweet and motherly. She even came to visit me in my dorm at college long after her son and I had broken up. And when he was in an awful waterskiing accident (can you say grand mal seizures?), she called me up late at night and found me curled up in the waiting room in ICU the next morning. Oh, what a mom-crush I had on her.

Later there was another self-absorbed boyfriend between husbands, whom I also *loved* with all my heart. He was my yoga instructor, and his mom was *precious*. She went hiking with us. Made blueberry pancakes. Had a rapper name (Mammo D, as in Yo Yo, I'm Mammo Deluxe). Hell, we even took her to Vegas to see Bette Midler on New Year's Eve with us. Kind of red flag when your boyfriend wants to spend New Year's Eve with his mom. *And* see Bette Midler. But guess what? So did I.

My second husband's mom died before we married, and my first husband's mom was not a kindred spirit. In fact, I never called her by her first name, even after fifteen years of marriage. Let's just say she was the daughter of a Baptist minister and leave it at that. She swore Jesus turned water into grape juice instead of wine, and she didn't consider me a Christian, because I hadn't been immersed. As if the water was magic instead of ceremonial. For the record, I'm a proud fourth-generation Presbyterian, the "chosen frozen." We sprinkle. We don't dunk.

As Gmamma famously said, "I don't need to be reborn. I got it right the first time."

That's the thing, Gmamma has a wry sense of humor. And sometimes we get tickled over the littlest things. And in those moments, it's almost as if we're related, mother and daughter, complicit in a private joke.

Laura Mansfield Spica
March 10, 2015 ·

GEEZER UPDATE: So I'm chillin with Gmamma at lunch yesterday, and this little sweet cotton top walks by. We wave and smile. She waves and smiles.

Let me interject here that we collect names as a hobby and have found some humdingers in the ole family tree. One particularly unattractive name from generations ago also makes us giggle. Like why would ANYONE EVER NAME THEIR DAUGHTER THAT?!?

Not that we've discussed this lately, you understand, but I wanted to give you some context for what happens next.

Gmamma leans over and says in a conspiratorial whisper:

"Guess what her name is?"

Me: "What?"

Gmamma: "Dorcas."

And we laughed till we cried because it's THE NAME we've always marveled at. I thought it was extinct like "Methuselah" or some other Biblical name, but DORCUS IS ALIVE AND WELL AND LIVING IN SHANNONDALE!

Our shoulders are going up and down as we try to contain ourselves, but the laughter keeps leaking out. Gmamma is like a naughty schoolgirl. "Thought that would grab you," she says with a triumphant smile.

Like · Comment · Share

👍 40 people like this.

Write a comment ...

And except for wondering aloud why I look so "broad of beam" in my blue jeans and not in a dress, Gmamma is not as hypercritical as she used to be. She's old and tired, and let's be honest here, she's virtually blind.

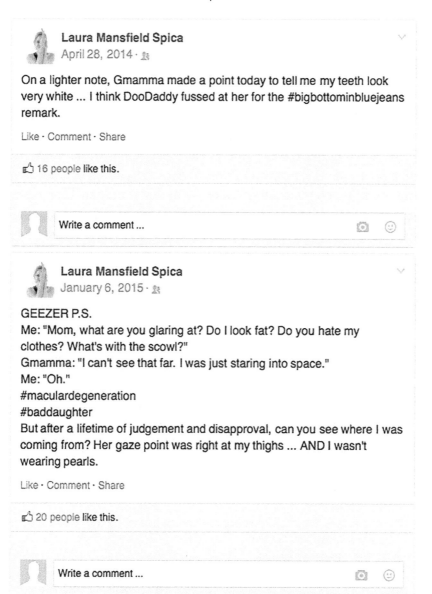

Laura Mansfield Spica
April 28, 2014 ·

On a lighter note, Gmamma made a point today to tell me my teeth look very white ... I think DooDaddy fussed at her for the #bigbottominbluejeans remark.

Like · Comment · Share

👍 16 people like this.

Write a comment ...

Laura Mansfield Spica
January 6, 2015 ·

GEEZER P.S.
Me: "Mom, what are you glaring at? Do I look fat? Do you hate my clothes? What's with the scowl?"
Gmamma: "I can't see that far. I was just staring into space."
Me: "Oh."
#maculardegeneration
#baddaughter
But after a lifetime of judgement and disapproval, can you see where I was coming from? Her gaze point was right at my thighs ... AND I wasn't wearing pearls.

Like · Comment · Share

👍 20 people like this.

Write a comment ...

Another favorite geezer and fantasy mom for me is Julia Pulliam, the Belle of Monteagle. Julia and her husband, Walter (pronounced "Waltuh") were Shannondale residents before Gmamma and Doo-Daddy. For my parents, they were a link to the good old days of elegant parties and bridge at the Club. Before moving to Geezertown due to Julia's Alzheimer's and Walter's advanced age (he was 101 when he finally died), the Pulliams lived in a penthouse on a private floor of Hamilton House, where they had knocked out the walls of three separate condos and extended their front door down the hallway to create a more spacious entrance hall. Julia always made all her own party food – dainty hors d'oeuvres and canapé – served by waiters from Cherokee who knew everyone's drink orders. Scotch neat for Gmamma. Bourbon with a splash for DooDaddy.

Julia is Southern to the core. A steel magnolia who survived the death of one of her two children. Divorced young, she married the middle-aged bachelor, Walter, who doted on her. They made Shannondale palatable to Mom and Dad. Ate their meals together, invited them to join their "Drinking Club." Julia wasn't allowed to use her kitchen, because she once put a pillow in the microwave.

Laura Mansfield Spica
September 6, 2014 ·

GEEZER UPDATE - WEEKEND EDITION:
Allow me to introduce Julia, the belle of Monteagle, and a lovely, lovely person. She is now suffering from Alzheimer's but has embraced it with her usual grace and aplomb. She resides at Shannondale with Gmamma & DooDaddy.
Overheard at the bridge table ...
Julia, with guileless charm in her thick Southern drawl, to her bridge partner, Chalmers, also afflicted with Alzheimer's: "Chalmers, do you know where you live?"
Chalmers, flummoxed and somewhat affronted by the inquiry: "Well ... do YOU know where you live?"
Julia: "No, I haven't any idea."
Chalmers, relieved and in a conspiratorial whisper: "Neither do I. They just drop me off here to play cards and then take me to a different hotel every night."

Like · Comment · Share

 30 people like this.

Write a comment ...

Laura Mansfield Spica
September 12, 2014 ·

GEEZER UPDATE: Since Friday is Bridge Day for Gmamma, DooDaddy and Julia, the Belle of Monteagle, I thought we'd listen in on a recent convo over breakfast. Julia is speaking to her husband, Walter (pronounced "Wal-tah"), who is 101 years old and sharp as a shiny new tack.
Julia: "Waltah, how old ARE you?"
Walter: "Julia, you know how old I am."
Julia: "No I don't."
Walter: "If you round up, I'm almost 200."
Note: Walter doesn't play bridge. The regular fourth was a delightful lady named Sarah, but she has been edged out of the Friday Foursome by a retired UT professor. Stay tuned ... #geezerdrama #icanteven

Like · Comment · Share

 26 people like this.

 Write a comment ...

~

 Laura Mansfield Spica
November 28, 2014 ·

Well, it's all fun and games till the ambulance arrives ...
And the firetruck (bless those firemen, Julie Luttrell Hinkle).
Fortunately, we had hot glazed from Krispy Kreme for those dear EMTs, thanks to a mid-dinner coffee run by Mac Bower. What can I say? Waltuh wanted coffee STAT.
It's taken me several hours to find the humor in Thanksgiving 2014, which will henceforth be known as the #GEEZERPOCALPYSE.
More later. Just got up to let Richard Parker out. For the second time.

Like · Comment · Share

30 people like this.

Write a comment ...

Laura Mansfield Spica
November 28, 2014 · 👥

Ok, so here's the morning-after update. After he adamantly refused to go to the hospital when the paramedics arrived, we took Waltuh and his lovely bride, Julia, the Belle of Monteagle, back to Shannondale. DooDaddy just now called to say Waltuh's condition worsened in the middle of the night, and he was taken to the ER. He is in the ICU now. Julia is frantic. Please send up some love & prayers today for this curmudgeonly gallant geezer, who regaled us with first-hand stories of WWII while he sipped his single-malt before his sinking spell. And for his precious, darling, demented wife, who will be lost without him.

Like · Comment · Share

👍 34 people like this.

Write a comment ...   📷 ☺

~

We had to take Dad's car keys away after he fell and broke his hip.

Dad's delusions about driving, despite his incapacity, remind me of his expectations for my mother, after she had double knee-replacement surgery. She never fully recovered her mobility, but Dad remained convinced that she could wear "pretty shoes" again and go dancing at the Club. It became an odd obsession for him—dressing her up and wearing her on his arm like a trophy wife. Not a new shiny version, but the same wife, aging gracefully, ever stylish, always appropriate. Like Grace Kelly if she hadn't died in that car wreck. Mom didn't want to wear pretty shoes anymore. Didn't give a damn. But it mattered to my father.

He was creating his wife in the image of Aunt Edie, the glamorous sister of his own mother, who died tragically young of tuberculosis. Aunt Edie *always* wore heels. Until the day she died at age 98. *Never* wore pants. Spoke with a Southern drawl as thick as the boiled custard for which she was famous. Dad told me that's how he coped with not having a mother. He simply projected all his

14

Laura Mansfield Spica
January 21, 2015 ·

GEEZER UPDATE: After visiting Gmamma and DooDaddy today, I went to see Julia, the Belle of Monteagle, who has now been moved to "the other side" of Shannondale. She's in Assisted Living, awaiting her move to Atlanta to be near her daughter. It will be a whole new world. Without Waltuh. Without her Knoxville friends and family. Without her bridge buddies who don't know what day it is but can still play some serious cards.

She's got a doctor's order for two oz. of Scotch each night, since she doesn't have access to the well-stocked liquor cabinet back in her apartment. No more happy hours and toddies. No more "Drinking Club" before dinner.

Julia is my hero. She is a plucky little geezer. Talk about steel magnolia. This gal is tough. Stiff upper lip. Elegantly resolute. And, through it all, still irresistibly charming and interested in other people.

"Laura, you will have to come this summer to Monteagle and bring your parents to sit on my porch and drink Scotch."

Indeed.

Like · Comment · Share

 50 people like this.

Write a comment ...

love and adoration and need for acceptance onto his Aunt Edie. He doted on her. Adored her. And she doled out the conditional love and constant criticism that characterized his childhood. And while I truly believe he loves his children with all his heart, it was hard for my father not to raise us the way he'd been raised, with a critical eye, trained to find faults to be corrected.

Aunt Edie taught fifth grade at the Robert E. Lee Grammar School in Fayetteville, Tennessee. To hear Dad tell it, she was wildly popular with the students, but I knew Aunt Edie, so I have my doubts. She never had children of her own. Married a wealthy widower when she was 40 after stringing along amorous suitors and breaking their hearts (picture Scarlett O'Hara at the Barbeque). Dad remembers how she would say to him as a child, "Why can't you be more like

Laura Mansfield Spica
May 9, 2014 · 👤

Stopped by Shannondale to see DooDaddy's long-lost half-sister passing through town with her recently acquired third husband. I ask about her daughter Patty, whom I vaguely remember from childhood. She points to a picture in the new wedding album she's brought for show & tell and says, "There's Patty. She's gotten fat."
And I think to myself, yep, this woman is a Mansfield alright.
And then I send up a little prayer that I will always see my child through #motherlove goggles instead of a magnifying glass.
Poor Patty. #blessherheart

Like · Comment · Share

👍 28 people like this.

Write a comment ...

Jack Willis (a classmate of his)? He's so handsome and smart." Or, "Why aren't you more athletic?"

I know this is anathema to my contemporaries, the doting parents of millennials, where every kid gets a trophy, and no one is ever made to feel less than worthy. But for a child of the Depression, raised in the South, by a gaggle of narcissistic women, like my dad was, unfavorable comparisons to other children were commonplace. Judgment was a given. And compliments were offered sparingly, so as not to spoil the child.

Dad always felt like he had to earn Aunt Edie's love, prove himself to his Kirby grandparents, and make sure they didn't regret taking him in, the little unwanted orphan boy, whose father was an alcoholic. Whose father later remarried and had another family but never sent for Dad. Whose father, a Mansfield, was never good enough for a Kirby girl in the first place. Maybe that's why my grandfather ultimately shot himself in the head, leaving Dad an actual orphan, rather than just an abandoned child.

"This boy needs a new suit," Dad's grandfather (aka Pappa) would say when he took my father shopping. "This boy" spoken in a Fog-Horn-Leg-Horn voice, I say, I say, this boy needs a new suit. It was the way he referred to Dad, instead of by name. I picture this man in a Colonel Sanders costume sipping a mint julep.

Pappa was a gentleman farmer, meaning he owned a farm and took Dad there to visit it from time to time. He got country hams from there at Christmas. But he didn't actually farm. Dad recounts scaring the fainting goats on Pappa's farm with his cousin, Billy Mansfield, and feeling guilty about it later. They would stiffen (the goats, that is). Then their eyes would roll back in their heads and they'd faint dead away, sure enough. What makes me smile is the thought that Dad felt terrible about it afterwards. Such a sweet little guy, this boy was.

Cousin Billy Mansfield later became an alcoholic and shot himself in the head. Well, in the mouth to be precise. Oh those Mansfield genes and those lost Mansfield boys. I worry about my own brother, another lost boy. Then again, maybe Cousin Billy just felt really bad about scaring those poor little goats.

So the "this boy" business wasn't a slight, per se, just an old man's idiosyncratic way of referring to his grandson. But Dad said he always worried that the folks at the men's store in Fayetteville would think he was some little urchin off the street, a charity case that his grandfather took pity on, rather than his actual grandson.

Not calling Dad by his name or claiming him as "my grandson" somehow implied that the generous old man buying the suit or paying for the haircut didn't even know the boy who would become my father. Dad just wanted to belong to someone. I wish I could go back and give that little boy a hug, sweep him up in my arms and tell him I love him and that he's the best boy in the world.

"It does something to a boy to grow up without a father," Dad once told me.

I guess he would know.

We were always told Dad's father died of a broken heart. But that never made sense to me. How does that actually work? Does your heart just stop beating from sadness? Or does it expand out of your chest like the Grinch who stole Christmas? So after the gazillionth time I asked about it, Dad blurted the truth out to me. That shut me right up. And broke my heart for my fatherless father and the childhood he never had.

And yet, I never quite felt like my father was real when we were growing up. He was gone, always gone. I dreamed once of trying to keep up with him in a crowd, running beside him on the sidewalk, his strides too long for my stubby legs. In the dream, I'm desperately reaching for his hand and when he finally takes it out of his pocket, it's a hook, rather than a hand. Like a pirate. Turns out, in my dream, the man I was frantically following wasn't my dad at all. It was someone else entirely.

~

When I was newly divorced from my first husband, Dad was my rock. Well into his second career of real estate, he found me a cozy rental house I called the Magic Cottage, where I entered my decade of single parenthood, while working full time at a demanding executive-level job for a perfectionist boss, who was never satisfied. Sound familiar? But I digress.

The particular memory I want to share is when I locked myself out of said Magic Cottage on my way to dinner with a friend. My young son was with his father that night. I called Dad, who also had a key. There was no emergency, no rush. I would get it from him on my way home from dinner. I wasn't three sips into my Chardonnay before Dad appeared at the restaurant, spare key in hand. Surprised, I looked up, "Dad I thought you were at the grocery store?"

"I was," he answered, breathlessly. "But you needed me, so I left my cart in the check-out line and came straight here."

I was slightly embarrassed by his over-attentiveness to his grown daughter. After all, I was no shrinking violet, no victim. I was a she-warrior, surviving a heart-breaking divorce and raising my child single-handedly. But to my father, I was his little girl in need. And he was going to save me. Whether I needed saving or not. And my friend, Carleen, who had daddy issues of her own, was enviously aghast and instantly smitten with Dad.

There's a duality to my parents, such a blatant contrast; it's hard to see what they ever had in common. People *love* my dad. Just like

Carleen. They are drawn to him, charmed by him, mesmerized by his charisma. My mother, on the other hand, is not so universally loved. She has a shrinking circle of childhood friends who are dying off. These people "get" Mom. They accept her and have a shared past of parties and privilege. I gather she was shy and studious as a child, lovely as a young woman, and a lot of fun before she was married.

I don't know how life disappointed her, but my mother changed somewhere along the way, or maybe she quit being the person she thought she should be and became who she really is. Tact is not her strong suit. She doesn't like to discuss things. Doesn't like to dwell on things. No sad movies. Nothing that might scratch the surface of real emotions. On the other hand, she loves animals, especially cats, and can recite Lewis Carroll and Shakespeare and the Bible with an impish twinkle. She adores my son, Mac, and my cat, Richard Parker.

Mom was a great lover of books, a voracious reader before macular degeneration robbed her of that passion. She used to paint and play cards. And in their early-married days, she and Dad both did Community Theater and "entertained" a lot.

 Laura Mansfield Spica
January 26, 2015 ·

Sooo Gmamma's got a BIG BIRTHDAY coming up. I asked DooDaddy how she'd like to celebrate. Let's listen in:
Me: "Dad, does Mom want to go to The Orangery for her birthday or have a homemade dinner at our house with chocolate ice-box pudding?"
[Please note that on Christmas Day, she was heard to remark in her Grumpy Cat voice "Where's the chocolate ice-box pudding?" It's my great-grandmother's recipe. Much loved by all. But we were having BRUNCH, so I didn't make it.]
DooDaddy: "Hold on. I'll ask her."
Sotto voce discussion offline while I wait on the phone.
DooDaddy: "She wants to go to Aubrey's."

Like · Comment · Share

 41 people like this.

Write a comment ...

19

It's like she was the original Stepford Wife. Playing a role. And finally, now that's she's old, she's not playing anymore. My father seems constantly amazed by this. He, who knows her better than anyone, doesn't really know her at all.

I remember Mom and Dad bickering about something when I was still a teenager living at home. "Why don't you just get a divorce?" I asked, seething with teen angst and exasperation.

"We don't *believe* in divorce," my dad answered for both of them. "We might move to opposite ends of the house, but we'll never get a divorce." And that's exactly what happened eventually. As I look back, it strikes me that he didn't profess his love for her or try to reassure me of the stability of their relationship. It was more about the institution of marriage. Till death do us part. And all these years later, they still bicker. Dad still picks at Mom and she snipes at him, but they are like Siamese Twins, inseparable, often incompatible, but conjoined for life.

Laura Mansfield Spica
July 21, 2015 ·

Ringalingaling ...
Gmamma (answering on the first ring): "HELLO? HELLO?"
Cousin Liz: "Jennie D., it's Liz."
Gmamma: "WHO?"
Cousin Liz: "Liz McClure, your first cousin, one of only two first cousins you have. I was your maid of honor at your wedding?"
Gmamma (hanging up the phone): "Well, you have the wrong number."
Click.
DooDaddy: "Who was that?"
Gmamma: "It was Liz."
#geezerlove

Like · Comment · Share

👍 31 people like this.

Write a comment ...

I distinctly remember my sixteenth summer. Elvis Pressley had died the year before, so it was the anniversary of his death. Hot. Sticky. August. My sister and I were in the backseat of Dad's Pontiac, driving up to White Pine, Tenn. Elvis songs playing on all three AM radio stations. *Wise men say only fools rush in,* he crooned and you couldn't help falling in love.

We were going to "sit" for our portraits. Oil portraits to be painted by Armande, who was staying with a childhood friend of our grand-mother's, Ellen McClung Berry, at her antebellum home, known as "Fairfax." I wore the dress my mother wore in 1957 when Aunt Ellen held a Confederate Ball as an engagement party for my parents. I swear I'm not making this up. It only now occurs to me that Armande probably wasn't even his real name.

So, my sister Keeling and I were up in an empty ballroom, draped over antique furniture, modern-day Southern Belles, acting out a role from a previous era. Not the Civil War, but my father's ideal-ized impression of my mother's privileged upbringing. And before I posed for hours in my mother's dress for Armande, Dad took me by the hands, and we spun around and around in circles, laughing until he accidentally let go and I fell hard to the floor. At the time, I thought it odd, that he was treating me like a very small girl, you know, when you twirl a toddler around, and her legs lift off the ground and she's flying. But later it seemed as though he was rec-reating me as my mother. She was no longer young and beautiful, and I was just coming into my own as his ideal blue-eyed blonde. Except my eyes are green.

Dad and I were in New York together a few years later. It was 1982, the year the World's Fair came to Knoxville. I remember, because all my friends were getting cool Fair-related jobs at places like the Stroh House, but I spent that summer on Martha's Vineyard, renting a house with seven other girls, working in a gift shop called The Golden Door.

Dad was traveling on business. I flew over from The Vineyard to meet him in Manhattan. We did the museums, had tea at The Plaza under Eloise's portrait. Saw a Broadway show, "Annie" I think, and had a sophisticated (it seemed to me) late-night supper somewhere. When we returned to his hotel, I remember having the distinct impression that the doorman thought I was my father's girlfriend. It was nothing Dad did, just gave me his arm as we walked in, but I felt suddenly ashamed. Years later, I would remember him describing how he took Mom to New York in the early '60s and how, when they walked in the theater, all heads turned to stare at my mother, chic, blonde and beautiful. And how proud he was to be with her.

You see, I realized early on that beauty was prized in my family— by my father, in particular. My sister was a precious little girl, all Shirley Temple ringlets and dimpled rosebud smile. Dad fondly remembers people stopping him and my mother on the street just to say how adorable Keeling was. But alas she grew to be a pudgy kid, in the sleek 1970s of Marcia Brady and Lauren Hutton and Charlie's Angels. This was *not* ok. Fat was just not as accepted as it is today. Keeling was forced to go on countless diets, restricted from certain foods. She dreaded pool parties where she might have to wear a bathing suit among her pretty, svelte peers. I was painfully skinny, all knees, ribs and elbows as a child, but it somehow sorted itself out in my teens. And suddenly, my father noticed me. Not in a sexual way, nothing like that, but as worthy. Because he thought I was beautiful. And beauty was power.

I guess when you grow up in a houseful of Southern girls in the 1930s, beauty is the ultimate power, to be wielded as a weapon, against the beauty-impaired. Louise, Josephine, Helen, Lillian, Edith and Laura. Aunt Helen was the ugly duckling, the old-maid schoolteacher, who never married and never fit in with her shallow, self-absorbed sisters. My father's mother, Lillian, looked like Zelda Fitzgerald. His father, Bo Mansfield, like F. Scott. They were the golden couple with the tragic ending, forever young and beautiful.

Dad recounts begging to not go to church on Mother's Day when he was little, because the ushers handed out roses to wear in your lapel—a red rose if your mother was living, as were all the lovely young mothers of every other child in Sunday School—and white if your mother was deceased. Dad hated being the only little boy with a white rose in his lapel. Lillian, his mother, was just a ghost, a pretty face in a faded photograph.

The three sisters who lived the longest and moved to Knoxville to figure prominently in my own childhood were Helen, Edith and Laura. Aunt Edie was, apparently, a beauty in her day, auburn-haired and full-figured, Marilyn Monroe-esque. By the 1970s, she seemed comical to me. Bright red lipstick, a dated hairstyle and a moonlight and magnolias accent, always criticizing my mother. My mother's housekeeping, her cooking, her every move. The tension was high when Aunt Edie came to visit. And Dad could not find it in himself to defend my mother against his own mother figure. I resented Aunt Edie for that. I resented Dad, too. While I could recognize and be mortified by my mother's shortcomings, I would have defended her to the death against Aunt Edie, with that butter-wouldn't-melt-in-her-mouth smile plastered on her powdered face, that geranium lipstick leaking into the tiny fissures around her mouth. Aunt Edie smoked, but she didn't inhale.

Even Aunt Helen jumped on the Mom-bashing bandwagon. She knew just how to turn a phrase and twist the knife at the same time. "Jennie D, I don't know how a girl as big as you can play tennis," she observed dryly. Kind of like saying "You don't sweat much for a fat girl," except there was no backhanded compliment, just the back of her sharp tongue to Mom's face with a stinging verbal slap. Sticks and stones break bones. But words can break your heart.

Dad swears Aunt Helen was just tactless and didn't mean any harm. Aunt Edie was less guileless, her barbs more pointed.

I was safe from Aunt Edie's contempt, because I was pretty. Or at least not fat. Once poor Keeling was actually jogging down the sidewalk on Kingston Pike when Aunt Edie pulled over and told her to get in the car so she wouldn't embarrass herself. Did I mention Keeling was wearing ankle weights, which she wore every day, even to school under her bell-bottoms, since Dad told her she needed to develop her calves?

When Keeling got a summer job at Shoney's, Aunt Josie (who had moved from Fayetteville to Mississippi and even deeper into the Deep South tradition of keeping up appearances and worrying what everyone else thinks) worried that Keeling's "reputation" would be ruined forever (pronounced for-EVAH). Working as a waitress. The very idea. Yes, Keeling was a disappointment to The Aunts.

Fortunately, my sister was kind-hearted, made good grades and was loved by her friends. And she had a lovely singing voice (as did Aunt Edie at one time), so she wasn't a total loss, in my father's eyes.

How well I remember Aunt Edie's warbling at the piano accompanying herself to "O Holy Night" in a voice that had long since lost all control of its vibrato. It was cringe-worthy. But if you glanced over at Dad, sipping bourbon, the wisp of cigarette smoke curling into a question mark from his lips, you'd think he was listening to Maria Callas at The Met—or maybe Mary Costa, because we like our divas blonde and blue eyed, don't we? And Mary Costa shopped at Watson's, the downtown department store Dad managed. He sold her a fur (pronounced FUH) coat. Natural mink. Female pelts, of course.

This is what we were dealing with growing up. My sister's weight yo-yo'd. My brother was bullied. And I went my own way, fearless middle child, having given up on being mothered, but still protective of my own mother, resenting my father, but, at the same time, wanting to please him. And then feeling guilty, because when my father's high beam of affection finally shined on me, my brother and sister suffered mightily.

I remember one time when Keeling lost 40 pounds. It was the same weight she gained and lost throughout her teens and early twenties. Tiny and small boned, like Dad's mother, Lillian, Keeling once ballooned up to 180 pounds. Or maybe it was 200. Meanwhile, Lillian stayed eternally young wearing pearls and Marcel waves locked safely in sepia-toned photos. Never aging. Never getting fat. Never losing her flapper-girl looks.

Once my sister came downstairs, wearing some party frock or other, feeling cautiously optimistic, hopeful in her newfound svelteness that she would gain Dad's approval and win his praise. She was modeling for Dad. An audience of one. The only one whose opinion mattered. I was on the couch in the living room, bearing witness.

Keeling walked in and tentatively twirled around in her sleeveless chiffon. Her neediness was palpable. Her eagerness to please reminds me of my dog, Henry, who will actually quiver with emotion as he seeks to meet my gaze. I don't remember Mom being there at all.

Suddenly, Dad clapped his hands together and exclaimed, "Kee, you look wonderful! Now all you have to do it firm up those arms. Then you'll be perfect in every way!"

He meant to be encouraging, he truly did. He didn't mean to damn her with faint praise of the you-don't-sweat-much-for-a-fat-girl variety. I didn't think anything of it at the time. Nitpicking people's appearances was a family sport. We'd watch the Miss America Pageant on TV just to point out the faults of the contestants. Miss North Carolina is knock-kneed. Miss Nebraska has horse teeth. It was years later, years of therapy for my sister, before she told me how that remark of our father's had crushed her self-esteem. How unloved she had felt. How judged and humiliated. And how she had carried it with her all her life.

"I know all about conditional love," said my dad. "I was raised on it." And so were we.

Keeling had a childhood friend, Dahl DeeBerry. Isn't that a great name? In my head, I spelled it "Doll." Dahl's mother always told her she was beautiful, and, therefore, she was. Dad was quick to point out that Dahl was actually plain—in fact, she wasn't even blonde. Long brown hair, brown eyes. Dull, dull, dull. No distinguishing features. Plain. Plain. Plain. #BlessHerHeart. But Dahl was the "It Girl" of Cheatum Park Elementary School in Springfield. All because her mother told her she was beautiful.

 Laura Mansfield Spica
November 14, 2014 ·

Most recent convo with Gmamma & DooDaddy revolved around Wheel of Fortune and how Vanna White's getting a little "long in the tooth." We all marveled at her telegenic longevity, but the #geezers wanted to know why in some dresses she has "no figure at all" but in other dresses she's looks quite "bosomy." #thatisall

Like · Comment · Share

 14 people like this.

 Write a comment ...

Dad would scratch his head at this and call it the "Dahl DeeBerry Effect." If you think you're pretty enough, then you are, even if you aren't. Pretty is as pretty does. He marveled at the ingenuity of Dahl's mother for thinking up this stratagem to instill confidence in her homely daughter. He had to hand it to Mrs. DeeBerry. Well played.

I don't think it ever occurred to Dad that maybe Dahl's mother really did see her as beautiful. And consequently, Dahl felt valued and loved and secure. And she projected that to other people with a quiet confidence. And isn't that what beauty really is? Self-assurance. Confidence. Feeling comfortable in your skin. Feeling loved and accepted just the way you are.

Chapter 2

Forgive Your Parents.

"Son, some things are better left unsaid."

–DooDaddy

Your geezers might seem helpless and harmless, and yet, they are still fully capable of wielding wicked skewers of emotional pain. You can't let your guard down and think of them like sweet, innocent children. They may be helpless, but they are not harmless. And, as usual, it's my sweet sister Keeling, who gets the brunt of it on her infrequent visits to Geezerville.

Now you might ask why Keeling still puts up with this bullshit. After all these years. I think it's because when you move away, your experience of your family of origin becomes frozen in time. All the "adulting" you do after you're gone just evaporates when you come home, and you're the same age you were when you left. With the same vulnerabilities and unresolved issues. I watch my sister revert to a former version of herself and take hit after hit like one of those sad, sand-filled plastic punching bags that pops back up every time you smack it down.

My brother, on the other hand, takes no shit from anyone. He's like Robert DeNiro in that scene from "Taxi Driver"—*You lookin'*

 Laura Mansfield Spica
March 18, 2015 ·

GEEZER UPDATE:
Well Gmamma was up to her old tricks on St. Paddy's Day.
She gave sweet Sister Keeling (visiting from Memphis) some green beads to wear around her neck. You know, the cheap plastic Mardi Gras beads you get at CVS? Kee donned them good-naturedly, and headed off to JC Penney to get DooDaddy a V-neck sweater for his upcoming birthday. Kee's sales clerk did not speak much English and was not wearing green, so Kee impulsively gifted him with the aforementioned dime-store beads, so he could participate in our peculiar festivities. Then she put on her cape and skipped back into the woods ... Cue ominous music here.
When she got home, Gmamma demanded to know where "her" beads were. She went on to explain, in no uncertain terms, that the beads were NOT Keeling's to give away and that she had only "lent" them to her. Keeling instantly reverted to the nine-year-old fat girl who just hid a spoonful of peanut butter in her drawer. She confessed everything and hung her head in shame. Gmamma then demanded that Kee return to JCP and retrieve the beads.
It gets worse ...
Instead of simply saying "Tut, tut, Gmamma, don't be silly," or, better yet, "LOOK, a squirrel," Kee GOT IN HER CAR AND DROVE BACK TO THE MALL. She proceeded to actually look for the sales clerk, who, mercifully, was no longer on the floor, in order to fulfill Gmamma's irrational order. It did not occur to my sister to just go buy some more beads at CVS. Or better yet to #justsayNO!
My sister is dear and kind and a pleaser. And there's just no pleasing Gmamma, never has been, even though she has mellowed into an impish, frail old version of her former fearsome self.
MORAL OF THE STORY: When you hear tales of elder abuse or #geezerbullying, don't always assume that the geezer is the victim ... and whatever you do, don't give away anything Gmamma "lends" you.
And be careful when you feed her. She might bite your hand.
#sisterlove

Like · Comment · Share

 🖒 38 people like this.

 Write a comment ...

28

at me? Just ready to knock someone's block off. And because he was the most vulnerable of all, he was wounded the deepest, in ways from which he cannot recover. Physically, he's fine. Emotionally, he's a ticking time bomb, ready to explode and spew shrapnel at any moment. Because he was the fatherless little boy my own father was. But instead of becoming a gregarious pleaser like our dad, my brother became a rage-filled workaholic. Well, they both share the workaholic gene. It's an excuse to avoid family obligations and a way to feel good about yourself at the same time. *I'm working hard to support my family, therefore I am a good person and a devoted family man.* Something like that.

When Randy comes home to visit, he gets hot under the collar, figuratively and literally. Gmamma and DooDaddy keep the heat way up, because old people are always cold. So Randy simmers, physically and emotionally, fielding long-distance conference calls from Europe, while Gmamma and DooDaddy tiptoe around him. Then he works out for hours at the local gym like a 'roid-raged nineteen-year-old. Finally his planned weeklong visit abruptly implodes after four days, when he just can't take it anymore.

You see, Randy has not yet learned Rule #1 for the Care and Feeding of Old People: Forget the past. Let it go.

My brother is great to have around though, because Dad listens to him in a way he doesn't listen to me. It's a gender thing. And because Randy works in medical devices, he's good with the docs and all the medical speak that's hard to process when you're sleep deprived from keeping a bedside vigil by your ailing parent.

Yet the one time he tried to approach Dad and tell him what happened all those years ago, explain why he's so angry all the time, why he's on his fourth marriage to his third wife, why he's estranged from his only child, Dad cut him off with the following one-liner that's right up there with his infamous "firm-up-those-arms" comment to Keeling.

"Son, some things are better left unsaid."

~

These days, Gmamma and DooDaddy are all about Keeling's frown mark. "Keeling sweetie, quit frowning," DooDaddy will say in an anguished tone, as he gapes brokenheartedly at the crevice between my sister's delicately arched brows (she has Grandmother Lillian's fine bone structure (pronounced struck-CHUH), thank the Lord. Those high cheekbones are her saving grace. Keeling will dutifully try to unfrown, which is hard for a 57-year-old-un-Botoxed woman.

Thank God I discovered Botox in my late '30s and erased that frown line for good. Also works on migraines and tension headaches, BTW. My dermatologist/Botox injector even remarks at the strong muscles in my forehead that resist even his most determined needle sticks. Bless Dr. Griffith's heart. He is my secret beauty weapon. I lie in Savasana on his examining table practicing Ujjayi Pranayama for pain control as he injects me over and over again. Nobody ever said perfection was painless.

Laura Mansfield Spica
January 2, 2014 ·

DooDaddy, upon receiving our Christmas card/wedding announcement that's been mysteriously lost in the mail for ten days: "Finally got your Christmas card yesterday. Not a very good picture of you."
Me, crestfallen, ever the pleaser after all these years: "Umm ... I thought my hair looked nice."

Like · Comment · Share

8 people like this.

Write a comment ...

My own firm-up-those-arms-and-quit-frowning moment came in my mid-twenties, as I was newly engaged to be married to my first (and only, I thought at the time) husband. He was much older (can you say father figure?) and had been married before. Twice, in fact. So we weren't planning a big wedding. Ironically, the date was October 29, the shared anniversary of both my sister and my parents, not for sentimental reasons, but because it happened to be UT's off weekend after the Alabama game in 1957, 1983 and 1988.

You don't schedule a wedding on a football Saturday in the South. It simply isn't done.

So Dad suggested I get a nose job. Yup. Rhinoplasty. The time was right, he explained helpfully, so I could get rid of my slightly bulbous nose (his Aunt Laura had the same nose, he offered up, taking the blame genetically, so to speak) in time for my wedding pictures. Then I would be perfect in every way. Mom, he pointed out, and Keeling, have The Perfect Nose. It's straight without a little gourd-like shape at the end. It's true. Their noses are perfect in every way.

Now friends, let me say here, I'd never had nose issues. If you look at my high school pictures and look at me today, I doubt you'll see any difference from my procedure. My metamorphosis was no Jennifer Gray from "Dirty Dancing" dramatic transformation.

Ironically, while Dad was offering up beauty advice, he wasn't offering to pay for it. So I opted for a partial nose job, which involved cartilage removal without actually breaking any bones (so it still has a bump and is not, in fact, straight and narrow like Mom's and Keeling's perfect noses). And it pulls to the left when I smile. So it was kind of a crappy nose job. Guess you get what you pay for. Elective surgery under general anesthesia, but without the black eyes. No biggie. Only a couple of days off work. Anything to please my father and make myself more perfect in his eyes.

The downside is that nothing lasts forever. I think noses are like the rest of your body, and they start to sag, bag and drag in middle age, so my nose looks a little droopy now. I'm paraphrasing Dolly Parton here, who famously said about her own plastic surgeries—"If it's saggin', baggin' or draggin' I get it nipped, sucked or tucked." Words to live by, I'd say. But then Dolly has always had a perfect nose. It might be the one part of her anatomy that has never been surgically altered.

And my nose whistles while I sleep. An unfortunate side effect of the cartilage removal, which caused the sinus cavities to collapse a little. Drove my between-husbands boyfriend crazy. Maybe that's why he ultimately cheated on me with two (that I know of) different married women. Or maybe he was just emotionally unavailable and incapable of true intimacy, like my parents. Are we seeing a pattern here? Choose partners you can never please, who are always just out of reach—like a hand in a pocket that turns out to be a hook. You're never quite good enough to hold that hand, and if you happen to grab it like the brass ring on a merry-go-round, that hand will let go of yours and you'll be lost again, in a swirl of faceless figures on a busy sidewalk.

Damn nose whistle. I bet Dolly Parton's nose doesn't whistle.

Laura Mansfield Spica
April 20, 2014 ·

Easter Dinner conversation at the Old Folks Home:
Gmamma: "Laura, you look so slim in that dress ... completely different from how you look in your blue jeans."
Doodaddy: "Goodness ..."

Like · Comment · Share

23 people like this.

Write a comment ...

~

When my siblings and I were very small, we lived for a time in a rented rancher in Middlesboro, Kentucky. I always thought the house was on Wesley Drive, but I've recently learned it was owned by a man named Wesley, which is why we referred to it as the "Wesley House." I remember the flatness of the yard matched the roofline of the house. I taught myself to ride my bicycle without training wheels in the backyard ... but that was later.

The time I'm thinking of, I was still a trike rider, because here's what happened: Keeling, Randy, and I were home alone. Mom had left a pot of spinach cooking on the stove. Frozen spinach was a staple of my diet, along with lettuce sandwiches, Tang and individually wrapped cheese slices. I was a big Popeye the Sailor Man fan and coveted his forearms. Besides, with enough salt, anything tastes good, even a frozen brick of spinach. This is a life truism that still holds today.

So the pot began to boil, the electric eye glowing an angry red. Smoke began to billow from the stove, and then there was the acrid smell of molten metal mixed with burned spinach. Keeling, still the leader of our trifecta at that time, gathered us up, and we made our escape. To the driveway. We'd never been farther than that by ourselves. So we pedaled furiously in circles singing, "Lady Bug, Lady Bug, fly away home. Your house is on fire and your children are all alone." Actually, that might be the soundtrack I've laid down in my head as I replay this memory. I don't think we sang anything. Just pedaled.

Mom and Dad must not have been gone too long, because, miraculously, they arrived home before the fire department got there. The house didn't burn down. And we had lumps of melted pot to play with in our sandbox. It was great fun. We'd bury them and then "discover" them over and over. Like panning for gold in the Klondike.

It was about this time I started telling my little brother Randy that Gypsies left him at our door and that Mom felt sorry for him and made him a bed in the sink. It always made him cry and tattle on me. I don't know why I did it. I loved Randy fiercely. Played with him for hours while Keeling was at school. There was no Mother's Day Out in those days. So I'd stand at one end of the flat lawn, up to my thighs in the tall grass and call for him like a beloved pet, "Come here, Little Buddy!" And he'd run as fast as his three-year-old legs could carry him, into my arms. We'd do that over and over till Keeling came home with her schoolbooks clasped importantly to her chest, her hair held back with a wide white plastic headband.

Randy and I would circle her hopefully, willing her to come outside and play. "I have to do my homework," she'd announce haughtily, leaving Randy and me stranded in our awkward pre-schoolness, in awe of her grammar-school grooviness. Randy would shrug it off and look adoringly back at me. His Big Buddy. And, this kills me to this day, I'd shun him and say I had homework to do, too (I didn't) and sashay off after Keeling, just hoping her second-grade sophistication would rub off on me. Leaving my Little Buddy behind, like a puppy. Abandoned. Vulnerable. Alone.

Our life was like a Peanuts episode back then. Parents were somewhere far away in the background, on the periphery of our childhood, the mwa-mwa-mwa of their voices droning in the background. There was lots of time to daydream, to stare up at the clouds, to lure ants with a tiny piece of my cheese slice as I sat on the back steps.

Mom made us popsicles by pouring grape Kool-Aid in plastic molds. It was a Tupperware thing, I think. And Keeling and I would sit on those same back steps, trying to suck the juice out of the ice before it melted down our arms and dripped purple dots on our matching dresses. Maybe Randy was napping somewhere inside, a lazy circular fan humming him to sleep.

My only memory of Dad from that era is of him mowing the yard and then racing us back to the house. He'd be pushing the mower, and we'd be running with all our might, but he'd still beat us. Because he was Superman. Invincible. Unstoppable. A force all his own. Funny that all my memories are of not being able to catch him.

It was along about then that Dad broke his hip for the first time. He was in a near fatal car crash. Had a terrible concussion and was in traction for weeks. We went to visit him in the hospital once, and he had a scruffy face. He looked scary. That was not our dad. I'd never seen my dad unshaven, much less bandaged and incapacitated. Mom was at the hospital a lot with Dad, I guess. So we stayed with Aunt Laura for some reason, instead of Grandmother. I don't remember why. But Aunt Laura made us chocolate cake, and I asked her if I could call her "Mommy." I'll never forget the look of surprise on her face. She mumbled something about me already having a mommy. I remember being disappointed that she didn't want to be my mommy. Either.

Dad came home to Middlesboro in an ambulance all the way from Knoxville, and we had great fun playing with his crutches, which seemed very tall to us. Mom would later say that Dad changed after the car wreck. That he was angry and mean instead of sunny and sweet. I don't know about that. I didn't really know him well enough to tell the difference.

Family lore has it that when he woke up after the crash, all he could think about was "Little Randy" as my brother was known back then. Dad was frantic that Randy had been in the car with him. "Who am I? What day is it? Where is Little Randy?" He kept asking this over and over.

Fortunately, my brother was not in the car in this seatbelt-less, pre-car seat era, or he would surely have been killed. I remember being glad Randy was safe but jealous that Dad only asked about him. I know now that love isn't a zero-sum game, that there can be enough to go around, but we were all so starved for attention from our absentee father and our detached mother that it sometimes seemed that way.

There was this awful conversation around the dinner table one night—I'm thinking we were probably having fish sticks and maybe Pop-Tarts à la mode for dessert. Mom was creative like that, with store-bought food. Somebody, probably me, asked who was Dad's favorite child. Pathetic, I know. I'm cringing as I write this. This is why I'm not needy now. I don't beg to be loved, and I don't set myself up for rejection anymore. Can't hurt me if I don't let you in, right?

So instead of reciting some parental cliché like, "You're all special in your own way, and I love you all just the same," Mom explained that Randy was Dad's favorite, Keeling was Grandmother's favorite, so I could be her favorite. I felt absolutely numb. Refused to accept it. Ran over to stand by Daddy (not Dad yet) and said that I wanted to be his favorite, too. I didn't want to be her favorite, whatever that meant. And in that moment, I experienced the twin miseries of rejection from my father and guilt for rejecting my own mother and whatever she might have had to offer me as her designated favorite.

When I was older, just to rub salt in my own wound, I asked Dad, hypothetically, if the house were on fire and he could only save one of us, who would it be? He answered without hesitation—Little Randy, of course.

And that pin in Dad's hip from the 1960s car wreck would come into play all these years later, when he fell in the dining room at Shannondale and shattered his femur. After the surgery, his X-rays looked like cartoons, with a giant screw holding his hip together from back in the day and a sleek new titanium rod running the length of his thigh, like the mercury in a thermometer.

My second husband once asked my father what he remembered about me as a child. I think he thought it would be fun for Dad to reminisce about his little girl.

"I really don't remember a thing," said DooDaddy.

Rule #2 for The Care and Feeding of Old People: Forgive your parents.

~

A psychic once told me my maternal grandmother was my guardian angel. That and there's a knee replacement in my future. But I already knew both of these things. Grandmother was an angel all her life. Among my fondest memories is making chocolate chip cookies with her in her apartment kitchen in Knoxville, standing side by side at the counter, aprons tied around our waists (mine was actually tied under my armpits). She'd let me measure everything out by myself. We'd also make a version with raisins in them (yuck) to freeze for when Uncle Billy came to town. And she'd save a child's fistful of chocolate chips in the bottom of the "little yellow bag," as I called the Hershey's chocolate morsels bag, for me to snack on while watching cartoons. I could make that bag last for hours, letting each individual morsel melt on my tongue. Savoring the bittersweetness.

Grandmother would read to me by the hour. I'd lie in her lap on her forest green sofa, and she would stroke my hair, putting it behind my ear as she read classic fairy tales and Bible stories. There was fringe on that sofa, and I'd pretend it was braided mermaid hair, running it through my fingers. Grandmother and I would memorize Bible verses and poems. I can still recite "Paul Revere's Ride" by Henry Wadsworth Longfellow. Also the Children's Catechism, the Lord's Prayer, and the 23rd Psalm.

Grandmother hand-smocked matching dresses for Keeling and me. Also flannel nightgowns with kittens on them. Well I remember Keeling trudging to breakfast in her flannel gown and cowboy boots so that one of our various cats couldn't spring out from under the sofa and pounce on her ankles. I thought it was a fabulous look.

When we moved back to Knoxville from Springfield, we'd go over to "Grandmother's House" for supper every Tuesday night and for

Sunday dinner after church. Dad would read the papers in the living room while I over-watered Grandmother's plants and helped her cook. Everyone else was noodling around doing something. These are the images I keep tucked away in a pocket of my heart. Happy. Family. Memories.

I still dream of Grandmother's house, which was actually a spacious apartment in what is now The Nicholas on Kingston Pike. Then it was the Mary Reed Apartments. She would take Keeling and me across the street to the Dulin Gallery (before there was a Knoxville Museum of Art) to visit the Thorne Rooms, miniature dioramas behind glass, tiny rooms preserved forever, perfect in every way. There were little stools to stand on for viewing. Keeling and I could stare at those rooms for hours.

Then we'd walk down the sidewalk on Kingston Pike, Keeling and me pretending to be blind, I'm not sure why. Grandmother would walk patiently behind us, wearing white gloves, silk stockings and low-heeled navy pumps, no matter what the season. This was her uniform. I assumed all grandmothers dressed like this. She wasn't a Granny, a Mimi or a Nanna and certainly not a Mamaw. Simply Grandmother.

Grandmother made the most amazing breakfasts. Full-on eggs and bacon every morning. She made toast in the oven, no toaster necessary, which is how I still do it. Real butter. Grape jelly. She let me save a tiny piece of bacon for a mousetrap I set every night in her kitchen. Kind of like leaving cookies and milk out for Santa Claus. My trap consisted of a book held up by a stick with the bacon underneath. Never did catch a mouse, but the trap was tripped and the bacon gone every morning. I thought Grandmother's mouse was the craftiest rodent ever. It just now occurs to me that Grandmother tripped it herself to keep the thrill of the mouse hunt going for me. This was when we still lived away, and Keeling and I spent our summers with Grandmother in Knoxville. When we left at the end of the summer, she'd promise to keep my trap set. Grandmother dutifully wrote me letters detailing Mr. Mouse's miraculous escapes.

During the years when we moved all the time, and I would wake up in an unfamiliar bedroom, I would always think I was at

Grandmother's house. My safe house. The only home I knew in those early years. Where else could I be? I can still smell the musty chintz pillows in the glider on the screened-in porch. If I close my eyes I can see Grandmother's silver thimble and the red pincushion in her sewing basket.

Grandmother still wrote with the kind of pen that you dip in a tiny jar of indigo ink. She let me play for hours with her dip pen, writing imaginary letters on the airmail stationery she used to write her son, my Uncle Billy, who was stationed in Germany at the time. I made a terrible mess. The underneaths of my nails were stained a dreadful blue hue that was nearly impossible to scrub out, even with a bristle brush. I just lapsed into Grandmother speak there—I don't think I've ever used the word "dreadful" in my life.

One morning Grandmother was up making breakfast, but it was way too early, still the middle of the night. She had gotten confused. This scared me. Grandmothers are reliable people who smell like talcum powder and who always know what's best. They should never be confused. They should always be certain of things. You see, I was not yet an expert in The Care and Feeding of Old People. I didn't know anything about heart palpitations and dementia. Grandmother was my beacon, my touchstone, my calm in the eye of life's storm.

I once found her dentures in a glass by the sink. She told me not to tell anybody. I later asked Mom about it. Teeth in glass? It was scary. Mom chastised me for telling. I felt ashamed. Like I had failed a loyalty test. Let Grandmother down.

She died suddenly of a heart attack on the sidewalk outside First Presbyterian Church where she had driven herself. She was wearing her usual navy-blue suit, pearls and pumps. She didn't suffer. I was in 7th grade. Got off the Webb School bus after school as usual. My friend Mary Helen had come home with me that day, thank goodness.

Dad was home from work, which was weird. He opened the front door as we were coming up the steps. He was just standing there with Mom, and he told me the news. I didn't really process it. Just escaped upstairs to my room with Mary Helen and sat there numbly. No one I knew had ever died before. While we sat there in our 7th grade sullenness, the door to my room opened suddenly and in walked Aunt Edie, of all people (without knocking, not cool). Dad was with her. She sashayed in, heels clickity clacking, stockings making a swish swish noise as her dimpled thighs rubbed together. Perfume and hair spray smells filled the air. Aunt Edie quickly expressed her sympathy and then got right to the point. She said something to the effect that since Grandmother was gone, she would be my grandmother now. Can't remember her exact words, but they were equal parts awful and inappropriate.

It was majorly awkward. I don't think I said anything at all. Neither did Mary Helen, but she provided a welcome buffer from my having to get up and hug Aunt Edie or respond in some other expected but insincere way. Dad and Aunt Edie turned and left after she had dropped that bombshell. Mary Helen and I exchanged a disgusted look. We were disgusted by everything back then, so this was not unusual, but it was exactly the support I needed at that moment.

And with that, the only grandparent I had ever known, my beloved darling white-haired grandmother was gone, but she has been with me ever since. My guardian angel. Bobby Drinnon, the psychic, recognized her immediately. And I dream of her still. The smell of bacon and eggs. The feel of cool starched sheets. My socked feet sliding on the dark hardwood floors. House plants in the windows. That little brown plastic watering can. The sound of traffic whizzing past on Kingston Pike below. It was a haven, this heaven on earth. Grandmother's House.

Gmamma, for all her apparent lack of sentimentality, still has the Wandering Jew plant that graced Grandmother's windowsill just above the cast-iron radiator. She tends it lovingly, and it continues to thrive 40-plus years after my grandmother's death.

Chapter 3

Don't. Throw. Anything. Away. Ever.

"You never know when you might need that."

–DooDaddy

I'm a very independent person. I've always taken care of myself. And others. Never really thought of myself as a control freak, but I'll own it if that means purging expired food from the fridge, compulsively fluffing pillows, and folding the laundry while it's still warm. I like order. I grew up in a house stuffed to the gills with stuff, like a pufferfish about to blow. Sterling silver, family portraits, and heirloom jewelry to be sure, but also 40 years of *National Geographic* and Mom's kitchen windowsill full of empty airplane-sized alcohol bottles. I'm not saying she drank. Or that she even traveled. She just kept things. Everything.

Folded and reused tin foil and scraped grease into an old Crisco can on the stove. Stacked and stashed brown paper grocery bags and

Laura Mansfield Spica
May 17, 2015 ·

Omystars, I can't even ...
Me: "Mom, have you been drinking your Ensure like Dr. Bhandari said to?"
Gmamma: "I tried to, but it tasted sour."
I dash to the fridge to find that the Ensure expired in 2013.
DooDaddy: "Oh, would you like those Polish hors d'oeuvres in the freezer for company?"
Me, via thought bubble: "WTF, Polish hors d'oeuvres?"
I open the freezer to find a bag of Polish potstickers from Sam's Club that expired in 2011.
Now I'm madly rummaging through everything in the fridge, finding a treasure trove of ptomaine poisoning. Did Gmamma and DooDaddy actually move expired groceries from the house when they came to Shannondale A YEAR AGO?
Why yes, yes they did.
Gmamma is laughing soundlessly, tears streaming from her eyes as I pull out a jar of pickles from 2008, yogurt & ice cream from 2014, Jimmy Dean frozen sausage biscuits from 2012, on and on it goes ...
"We thought we'd be snacking in the apartment a lot more, " explains DooDaddy, "But we really eat all our meals in the Dining Room."
Me, via thought bubble: "THANK THE GOOD LORD!"
I left them with bottled water, Powerade, and the candy from Gmamma's Christmas stocking. I confiscated Girl Scout Cookies (From this year not last year. I checked.) to take home with me. It would be a tragedy to let Samoas go to waste. I did leave a half-eaten roll of Thin Mints in the butter dish. And half a Rueben sandwich in a paper bag from yesterday's lunch, but only because Gmamma had carefully labeled it "May 16, 2015."
I should have wondered why they didn't need me to buy the Ensure, why they kept saying they had some in the fridge.
Does Powerade have a shelf life?
#iliterallycanteven
#GeezerGold

Like · Comment · Share

 51 people like this.

 Write a comment ...

recycled Christmas wrapping paper. Children of the Depression were the original green generation, repurposing and "upcycling" before it was a thing. My parents were alike in that way, still are.

"After all, you never know when you might need that," DooDaddy points out, as rationale for never throwing anything away.

In their elegant geezer apartment at Shannondale, the sofa and the dining room table are completely covered with junk mail, *National Review* magazines and dog-earned Talbot's catalogs. DooDaddy is always on a quest to find Gmamma the perfect red blazer. It's the old retailer in him and his need to dress Mom like a compliant doll into his version of what a geriatric Stepford wife should look like. Must. Keep. Up. Appearances. Aunt Edie and her sisters may be gone, but they still exert a great deal of influence.

So you can see why I "art direct" my pantry shelves and stage the toothbrush cups and Q-tip holders by the bathroom sink—it's a reaction to the clutter that engulfed my childhood. The mindless accumulation of things. I like surfaces. Uncluttered. I'm a ruthless thrower outer. If I buy a new item of clothing, I get rid of something in my closet. Excess stuff makes me claustrophobic. It's just one manifestation of my own perfectionistic tendencies. A place for everything and everything in its place. It soothes me to have clean sheets on the bed and fresh vacuum marks on the carpet.

Ahh, the satisfaction of arranging my blouses and sweaters by color and sleeve length. And am I the only one who hangs artwork on the walls of her closet? I think not …

Feng Shui is my Zanex to escape the physical chaos of my childhood and its suffocating surroundings, to cast off the dust and detritus of my past.

Rule #3 for The Care and Feeding of Old People: Don't. Throw. Anything. Away. Ever.

~

So, you can see I fail miserably at this one. Gmamma calls me The General, as I efficiently organize things to military precision. But stuff matters when you're old. Geezers develop a need to "gift" people with their old clothes as a way of carrying on. An antique broach, a tweed jacket, a cashmere sweater or, that most sacrosanct totem of all—Mom's full-length mink coat. All these gifts must be accepted with grace and then dutifully worn when you visit your geezers, to show you value their old clothes as much as you value them. Because these items are an extension of self, imbued with mystical qualities and eternal life. It's an I-may-be-dying-but-my-clothes-live-on kind of attitude. Don't try to understand it. Just embrace it. You will make a geezer's day if you show up for lunch in the dining room of the retirement home wearing a hand-me-down item of clothing and vintage jewelry. I promise.

And if you do have to bring a dumpster to the driveway of your childhood home and purge all of your parents' cherished belongings, make sure they've left the premises. Mom walked regally down the sidewalk and never looked back. It was as if she was afraid she might turn into a pillar of salt.

Laura Mansfield Spica
April 7, 2014 ·

It's the night before the BIG MOVE so I call up DooDaddy and he answers all outta breath ...
Me: "Whatcha doin? Are you ok?"
DooDaddy: "Yes, I've been bringing Gmamma's old evening dresses downstairs from the back closet so we can decide which ones to take."
Me: "Dad, you do realize she's on a walker, right?"

Like · Comment · Share

👍 25 people like this.

Write a comment ...

~

I've moved five times in the last 20 years. And I've left behind a piece of my heart in each house I lived in and loved. I can only imagine how hard it was for Gmamma and DooDaddy to leave their home of nearly 50 years to move to a "retirement community," as nursing homes are euphemistically referred to these days.

Actually, DooDaddy would take great exception to the term, "nursing home," because he and Gmamma still live on their own (sort of) in an apartment within the three-tiered complex. The next tier is called "assisted living" and the final tier—with wheelchair zombies parked in the hallways—the dreaded nursing home.

Two years ago, Gmamma fell on the front walkway on her way to the mailbox and broke her tailbone. This was after DooDaddy fell on the same walkway on his way to the same mailbox and tore his quadriceps tendon. Gmamma lay peacefully in the grass until DooDaddy called the fire department to come get her up. It's like the cat-in-a-tree thing but with old people.

DooDaddy was not so lucky when he fell. It was raining cats and dogs—maybe even armadillos—when he went down. Because Gmamma is deaf, she didn't hear him yelling for help or notice him crawling up the front lawn like the girl in the Andrew Wyeth painting ("Christina's World." Google it). With great effort, he dragged himself, sopping wet, up the front steps in excruciating pain to bang futilely on the front door.

Gmamma was watching "Jeopardy" with the volume on high. An atomic bomb wouldn't have budged her. Only when the neighbor across the street called Gmamma (and 911) did my mother realize what had happened. Thank you, sweet Mary, for always looking out your window.

A couple of months after she broke her tailbone, Gmamma had a stroke. The EMTs had to carry her down the stairs and out the front door buckled into a special chair contraption, because they couldn't get a stretcher up to her bedroom.

Old Sequoyah Hills homes are death traps for the elderly. There are treacherous slate walkways and creepy basement steps, skinny hallways and hilly yards to navigate. But DooDaddy had promised Gmamma she could leave "feet first" and that he would never make her move to the Old Folks Home.

Never. Say. Never. This could be a whole 'nuther stand-alone rule for The Care and Feeding of Old People.

I had to call in the Big Guns, my little brother, who is highly respected by the geezers, to convince DooDaddy that he could no longer honor his promise to our mother. And that if anything ever happened to him, she'd be making that journey alone. Gmamma relented grudgingly, like Granny Clampett in her rocker strapped to Uncle Jed's truck.

Gmamma says now she has no memory of the move. I sequestered her at my house when the movers came, so she wouldn't have to watch the dismantling of her family home. As we walked slowly out the front door for the last time, Gmamma didn't look back.

DooDaddy, who was still walking independently and driving back then, nearly killed himself bustling Gmamma's furs (pronounced "fuhs") and evening gowns to the car. He forgot his own raincoat in the hall closet. But artwork and jewelry, silver and scrapbooks made the move. All the inessential essentials.

My dear friend Morena, lovingly decorated the new apartment mirroring the color palette of the house in Sequoyah. Now Gmamma and DooDaddy sit in their transplanted living room chairs, comfortable and content as house cats, napping off and on all day. Their space is sacred. They are home. They are together, like matching bookends on a shelf, holding the precious stories of their shared existence.

And my brother, sister and I have peace of mind knowing the nurses are administering our geezers' myriad of medications and are on call 24/7 in case of a seizure, stroke or fall. And the mailbox is just down the hall.

~

DooDaddy is a dapper dude. My buddy Jamie calls him a "fine gent." Let's just say he was a metrosexual before it was a thing. But not in a foppish way. He's not given to pinkie rings, decorative pocket squares or novelty socks. DooDaddy's more of a cashmere V-neck, camel hair blazer kinda guy. And back in the day, he could flat out rock some plaid wool trousers at a holiday party. I seem to remember a powder blue ruffled tuxedo shirt back in the '70s, although I've tried to block it out.

You see, my father's first career was in retail. During our early childhood, he was with J.C. Penney, and we were transferred all over the place—I lived in six different houses in five different cities before the age of seven.

When DooDaddy joined Watson's, we were able to settle back in Knoxville, my mother's hometown. Watson's on Market Square was a happening place in its heyday. And DooDaddy was the host of that particular party, greeting customers every day and dressing them in salvage stock designer clothes and luxurious mink coats (female pelts preferred). Once the touring company of the Moscow Ballet swooped in and scooped up 26 full-length minks to take back to the Soviet Union.

There were Vera Wang wedding dresses, Hickey Freeman suits and Diane Von Furstenberg wrap dresses, also antique oriental rugs and crystal chandeliers—all at fire sale prices. You never knew what treasures you'd find, particularly in the Bargain Basement. My brother, sister and I all worked stints at Watson's over the years, on the floor as well as gift wrapping and doing inventory, and, in my case, modeling fur (pronounced "fuh") coats with my friend Debbie, traipsing up and down Market Square. But I digress.

DooDaddy and Gmamma left the old homestead in a bit of hurry, since it sold in a week. DooDaddy brought along armloads of Gmamma's evening dresses but forgot everything in the hall closet when they

refugeed to the Old Folks Home. So we've been gradually replenishing his wardrobe. Last year it was a handsome topcoat. This year it was a leather jacket. Oh the trials and tribulations of shopping with geezers. Lord have mercy! Don't get me started on trying to buy granny panties for Gmamma. I literally can't even.

The quixotic quest for the perfect leather jacket (not too heavy, caramel or chocolate brown but not black, with no zippers, fringe or other embellishments) took

46

me to three different stores, special ordering (and then returning) two different jackets, and finally buying six coats on approval and schlepping them over to Shannondale. Because finding a geezer chair in the middle of the men's department during a sale is tricky. As is donning and doffing jackets while holding on to your walker.

Remember Old Age is a full-time job. You can't just clock out for a shopping spree.

However, I think you'll agree that the final selection (at 30 percent off) is the perfect choice for DooDaddy.

Buttery soft, elegant lambskin in a warm chocolate brown, just right for a leisurely stroll. On a walker.

Chapter 4

Food Matters. A Lot.

"All cookies are good. Some are better."

–DooDaddy

Y ou'd think by the time you're 85 or so years old, you wouldn't

Laura Mansfield Spica
October 20, 2014 ·

Me: "What did you have for lunch?"
DooDaddy: "Fried chicken and vanilla ice cream with chocolate sauce. You know, simple food."

Like · Comment · Share

👍 19 people like this.

Write a comment ...

really care what you eat. Chances are your teeth are shot, and your mouth is full of elaborate dental work like the grid of a skyscraper—bridges, caps, partials, veneers—or maybe you've had 'em all pulled and you're sporting dentures. My parents never had dental insurance, but that didn't stop them from undergoing expensive and painful gum and teeth work. DooDaddy has a regular dentist, a periodontist, and an oral surgeon in his little black book.

Nevertheless, he can wax poetic about breakfast. It's the highlight

 Laura Mansfield Spica
October 23, 2014 ·

#TBT all the way to yesterday. Wednesdays are now #GeezerWednesdays, as I am devoting them to the care & feeding of my favorite old people. I arrived shortly after breakfast. Let's listen in ...
Me: "What did you have for breakfast?"
DooDaddy: "My FAVORITE breakfast with VERY. CRISP. BACON."
Gmamma: "What did he say?"
DooDaddy: "One egg over easy on toast. Prune juice. And a doughnut, just for fun."
Gmamma: "What's he saying?"
DooDaddy: "And those little squares (hand motions here) ... Those little squares"
Me: "Ummm ..."
DooDaddy: "Those little squares of cereal that are iced ..."
Gmamma: "Frosted Mini Wheats!"
Me: "I thought you liked Honey Nut Cheerios?"
DooDaddy: "I do, but I was taking a break."
DooDaddy: "And about half the time we split a banana ..."
Me: "You split half a banana?"
DooDaddy: "No we split a WHOLE banana about HALF the time. But HALF the time we don't even HAVE a banana."
Gmamma: "Doughnuts are supposed to be greasy."
Me: "Yeah, dry cakey doughnuts are the worst."
Gmamma: "What'd she say?"

Like · Comment · Share

 25 people like this.

 Write a comment ...

of his day. As I write this, we're in the hospital for yet another TIA/ stroke/seizure, and he's tucking into his breakfast tray. "I have trouble eating dry eggs, because they fall off the fork," he complains, barely pausing for breath before lifting another forkful to his mouth. He's making do, despite the dryness of the eggs.

But oh, the glory of Breakfast At Shannondale—like manna in the desert for the Israelites.

Maybe it has to do with being Southern and food being such a big part of our culture. Every family gathering happens around food. Holidays, weddings, funerals, parties, it's all about the food, which becomes another benchmark of female perfection. Aunt Edie was known for her boiled custard and Aunt Laura for her chocolate wet cake. If you weren't an accomplished hostess, you were a failure in the Southern society of my parents' world.

And there were stories about young matrons not getting into the Junior League, because they made their chicken salad with dark meat.

For geezers, food becomes the connection to their past lives, the smells and tastes of happier, healthier times before old age and diverticulitis and diabetes. The good old days when you could eat whatever the hell you wanted and not be up all night with indigestion.

And growing up during the Great Depression meant doing without and making do for my parents. Food was not something to be taken for granted. Later, during World War II, you ate your Spam sandwich and were grateful for it. It was the patriotic thing to do, like planting Victory Gardens.

During my own childhood, the waste-not-want-not philosophy was strictly upheld. We were constantly admonished to think of the starving children in Africa when we didn't clean our plates. Except for my sister Keeling, who was supposed to eat less instead of more. In her case, social responsibility was at odds with the mandate to be thin, and thin was more important than the African children.

We didn't eat out much when I was growing up. Mom made her standard fare, baked chicken on the bone, white rice and canned green beans (with slivered almonds if she was feeling fancy). We had more than our fair share of TV dinners, too, on our own personalized TV trays. Libbyland TV Dinners—with macaroni and cheese and burned chocolate pudding that scalded the back of your throat on the way down—were an iconic meal of the '70s. Served up to a Friday night line-up of "The Brady Bunch" and "The Partridge Family." Before Libby's Libby's Libby's on the label label label, there was astronaut food—Tang and space food sticks. Also Cap'n Crunch, Lucky Charms, Twinkies, bologna on white bread, Diet Rite, Fresca and Tab. My childhood menu was a happy smorgasbord of sugar, fat and preservatives.

 Laura Mansfield Spica
September 10, 2015 ·

The grey goose is back in his nest. Meds tweaked. Will be adding a cardiologist to our list of specialists (see earlier posts about slate man and tailor). Bottom line, you can't keep a good geezer down. Because #DooDaddy
Best convo from the hospital that had the nurse in stitches (the good kind):
DooDaddy: "But why does the doctor want me on a low-carb diet? I'm not fat."
Pregnant pause. Nurse and I try to contain our impending convulsions as we exchange bug-eyed looks.
DooDaddy, glancing down at his rotund, Santa-like middle, "But I guess I'm not really thin either."
Nurse/DooDaddy/Me: BWAHAHAHAHAHAHA!!!!!

Like · Comment · Share

 54 people like this.

  Write a comment ...

After his umpteenth TIA/seizure/spell, DooDaddy was instructed to go on a low-carb diet and give up his beloved breakfasts and desserts. It was like you'd popped all the balloons at a kid's birthday party. He was thoroughly dejected.

Fortunately, Dr. Johnson, DooDaddy's long-time internist nipped the restricted diet plan in the bud, basically paraphrasing Gmamma's needlepoint pillow. Life is short. Eat Dessert First. He told Dad to eat whatever he wanted, including his beloved eggs and *very crisp bacon* breakfast.

It was like a Get-Out-of-Jail-Free card and Christmas morning all rolled into one.

Laura Mansfield Spica
February 11, 2015 ·

GEEZER UPDATE: Gmamma opined that she'd like to try a Bojangles Cheddar Bo. Well, she can cross that off her bucket list now. And on a scale of 1-10 she gives it "about a 9." #winnerwinner

Like · Comment · Share

👍 23 people like this.

Write a comment ...

Gmamma is literally wasting away. She's loses five pounds every time we go to the doctor (oddly enough, I'm finding those lost pounds and sticking them to my hips with Velcro). After picking on her to lose weight for the past 57 years, DooDaddy finds himself in the unfamiliar role of Boost pimp, Ensure pusher, peddler of Babybel cheeses. Anything to stabilize Gmamma's weight. He and Gmamma are like Jack Sprat and his wife in reverse.

My mother still likes ice cream. It's genetic, and it might be the

Laura Mansfield Spica
September 26, 2014 ·

On the way to the doctor with Gmamma. We pass Calhoun's ...
Me: Ooo I need to make some chicken chili, you know that white chili they have at Calhoun's? Would you like me to bring you some?
Gmamma: I don't like chili, any kind of chili. Chili is for the birds.

Like · Comment · Share

👍 23 people like this.

Write a comment ...

one gene I didn't inherit from her. "McClures love ice cream," Doo-Daddy explains, referencing Gmamma's side of the family, as she waits patiently for her monkey dish of Moose Tracks after every meal.

The good news, from DooDaddy's perspective, is that Gmamma can wear all sorts of clothes she hasn't been able to wear in years. She has a bather come in once a week (I was the bather until someone died, and this highly-coveted personal caregiver had an opening). Janie Moon has been working at Shannondale for 30 years and looks like a cheerleader, according to DooDaddy. She not only helps Gmamma take a shower, she goes through the closet and dresses her up like a Barbie Doll, coordinating scarves and sweaters and skirts. So all this wasting away has its benefits. DooDaddy once more has an elegant svelte blonde on his arm—or at least on the walker next to him as they promenade down the halls of the retirement home. You can never be too thin or too rich, right?

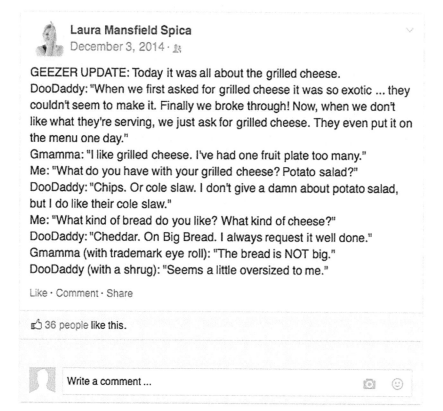

Laura Mansfield Spica
December 3, 2014 ·

GEEZER UPDATE: Today it was all about the grilled cheese.
DooDaddy: "When we first asked for grilled cheese it was so exotic ... they couldn't seem to make it. Finally we broke through! Now, when we don't like what they're serving, we just ask for grilled cheese. They even put it on the menu one day."
Gmamma: "I like grilled cheese. I've had one fruit plate too many."
Me: "What do you have with your grilled cheese? Potato salad?"
DooDaddy: "Chips. Or cole slaw. I don't give a damn about potato salad, but I do like their cole slaw."
Me: "What kind of bread do you like? What kind of cheese?"
DooDaddy: "Cheddar. On Big Bread. I always request it well done."
Gmamma (with trademark eye roll): "The bread is NOT big."
DooDaddy (with a shrug): "Seems a little oversized to me."

Like · Comment · Share

🖒 36 people like this.

Write a comment ...

Early in their confinement, I visited the geezers for lunch and was held captive, like a deer in the headlights, by a woman called Ernestine. She wanted to know everything about me. She stood very close, so close I could see the lines of mauve lipstick bleeding up from her lips. She spit a little at me as she spoke. Not egregiously, just consistently. Ernestine told me about her children, her son the dentist, her other son the lawyer and all her grandchildren. She had meticulously-dyed jet-black hair and pearls the size of gumballs circling her frail neck and nestling in the deep pocket between her collarbones. It was hard to look away, to disengage, but I had to, in order to converse with my own parents. You feel guilty not giving geezers all the attention they crave. But it's draining, and you have to conserve your energy.

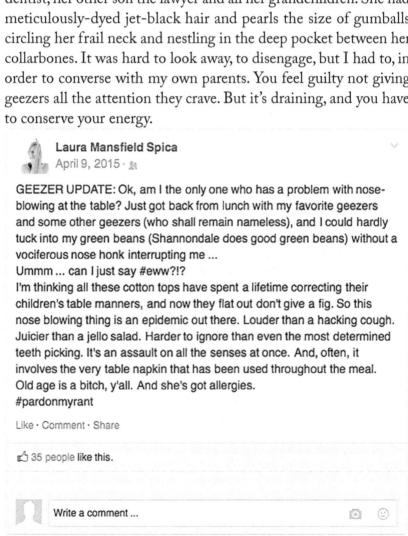

Laura Mansfield Spica
April 9, 2015 ·

GEEZER UPDATE: Ok, am I the only one who has a problem with nose-blowing at the table? Just got back from lunch with my favorite geezers and some other geezers (who shall remain nameless), and I could hardly tuck into my green beans (Shannondale does good green beans) without a vociferous nose honk interrupting me ...
Ummm ... can I just say #eww?!?
I'm thinking all these cotton tops have spent a lifetime correcting their children's table manners, and now they flat out don't give a fig. So this nose blowing thing is an epidemic out there. Louder than a hacking cough. Juicier than a jello salad. Harder to ignore than even the most determined teeth picking. It's an assault on all the senses at once. And, often, it involves the very table napkin that has been used throughout the meal. Old age is a bitch, y'all. And she's got allergies.
#pardonmyrant

Like · Comment · Share

👍 35 people like this.

Write a comment ...

Rule #4 for the Care and Feeding of Old People: Food matters. A Lot.

 Laura Mansfield Spica
September 3, 2015 · 🔒

And what do you bring from Alaska for the geezer with the discerning palate? Why, smoked salmon pâté of course ...
#geezerlove

Gmamma and DooDaddy generally take their meals with Ron. He's suffering from progressive supranuclear palsy and is losing his ability to swallow. Consequently, he makes indelicate sounds at the table, while choking on his food. This unfortunate habit apparently drives Gmamma crazy. But Ron's a whiz at the bridge table. Remembers every card. So he has earned Gmamma's respect. Once when I offered to fill in a foursome, Gmamma replied scornfully, "Better take some lessons first." I was not worthy.

"I do wish Ron wouldn't insist on ordering corn muffins," DooDaddy opines. "They're hard to swallow in the best of times."

Ron wears a chain around his neck with bib clips to secure his napkin in place and catch the inevitable spills and drips. DooDaddy jumped online and ordered one for himself on Amazon. He wears it in solidarity with his friend.

~

Today we continue the culinary adventures of DooDaddy with a visit to an old favorite: Wright's Cafeteria. You don't have to go all the way to East Knoxville for Southern soul food—look no further than Middlebrook Pike, just down the road from The Old Folks Home. It's open every day for lunch and Thursdays for supper.

We used to go to Wright's all the time when my son was little. This was in my previous lifetime, my first marriage. Gmamma and DooDaddy would meet us there (still driving then, still living independently). I was able to trick my toddler into eating chicken livers for a time because they looked like Chicken McNuggets, but he soon wrinkled his tiny nose in displeasure and opted for blue Jell-O, fried okra and big yeasty rolls. We used to send Christmas cards of Mac to the servers at Wright's, and they would put them up on the wall behind the counter. So when my marriage ended, I closed the chapter on Wright's and turned the page. Too many happy memories turned bittersweet. I also didn't eat Skittles for years or go to Long's Drugstore on Saturday mornings for post-soccer pancakes. Too many memories.

The other day, DooDaddy and I arrived at Wright's, and it was like nothing had changed in a decade. The same people were eating at the same tables. DooDaddy had Old Home Week with several cronies. And there was David Wright, frozen in time, still serving up chicken livers in his white apron. He hadn't aged a day. It was like a trip in the Wayback Machine, except Gmamma wasn't there.

DooDaddy happily tucked into his turnip greens, sweet potatoes and, of course, chicken livers with gravy, topped off with a piece of butterscotch pie (good, not great, DooDaddy declared, but he ate it every bite). I went with a deviled egg ('cause I miss my mother's homemade ones) and a tossed salad with about a gallon of housemade blue cheese dressing and, of course, fried okra, for all the noms. They'll carry your tray for you, so no worries if you're on a walker. And where else can you feast on down-home cookin' for just under $20?

My father called me up that evening from the dining room at Shannondale.

DooDaddy: "Sweetie, I can't remember what we had for lunch. I was telling my dinner companions, and all I can think of is chicken livers. Can you remind me?"

Me: "Turnip greens, sweet potatoes with marshmallows and butterscotch pie with real meringue."

DooDaddy: "Oh that's right. Wright's always does the best meringue."

I was telling a friend of mine later that it was like lunch was the highlight of my father's day. My friend suggested that it wasn't lunch but spending time with his daughter was the highlight of my father's day.

"That's it exactly. How do you know DooDaddy without ever meeting him?" I asked.

"I know his daughter," he replied.

~

This year, when Gmamma said she'd like to eat sliders for her birthday, because she'd seen them advertised on TV, I first had to clarify that she meant those mini-hamburgers that are ubiquitous in sports bars. Yup. That's what she wanted—birthday sliders. Her electric blue eyes lit up at the very idea!

My Facebook community was helpful with recommendations ranging from upscale (Cru) to low-brow (Krystal) and everything in between. I did my own research, calling LongHorn Steakhouse (after scouting their flat, geezer-friendly parking lot), but their sliders are shaved prime rib. Too fancy. DooDaddy suggested Applebee's, but when I called to inquire, they said they no longer served sliders. They were on to the next trendy pub grub.

I even sampled sliders at an after-hours business gathering at Crown & Goose, a geezer favorite, but they were like bocce balls on buns. Didn't cut the mustard (pun intended and borrowed from my fellow slider taster, Sharon).

We finally settled on Ruby Tuesday, after vetting their sliders as not being blackened, BBQ or otherwise too exotic for Gmamma's discriminating palate. She's like Mikey on the old Life cereal commercials. She hates everything. But no indeed, they were actual burgers, two to a serving, with a fried pickle skewered on top and a side of fries.

So the geezer family road trip was on, despite the snowflakes swirling and the fierce wind blowing. We piled in Joan Jetta, walkers tossed in the trunk and geezers buckled safely in the front and backseat. Gmamma was heard to remark as we disembarked from the vehicle, "People are gonna wonder why you got us old people out on our walkers in this weather."

For birthday sliders, of course! And because 90(ish) is the new 80.

~

Always up for a culinary adventure, DooDaddy was eager to try the hot chicken at Jackie's Dream, the soul food mecca on McCalla Avenue. So we picked up Cousin David, DooDaddy's uber-hip, downtown-dwelling, of-the-moment foodie and first cousin, and headed to East Knoxville.

DooDaddy artfully dodged some dangerous potholes in the parking lot as he steered his walker in the door of what looks like a juke joint on the outside and smells like Heaven when you open the door.

One look at the menu of Southern comfort food, and DooDaddy was home.

As we pondered the selections, debating the merits of collard greens over fried okra, yams versus mashed potatoes and cornbread or rolls (why not both?), our conversation inevitably turned to politics. The Republican debate the night before had sunk to new lows with Lil' Marco and Lyin' Ted ganging up on Big Donald. Mitt Romney had just jumped on the Trump-bashing bandwagon, perhaps angling for a pivotal role in a brokered convention.

One thing I have always loved about my father is his open-mindedness and his willingness to see things from all sides. When I was growing up, we had lively discussions about politics and religion around the dinner table (although the meals were not as mouthwatering as Jackie's—Gmamma didn't do fried). DooDaddy would give his opinion, and then I'd ask him for the counterpoint. He'd oblige me and give an equally articulate summation of the other side of the argument. He would have made a fine attorney, courtly and eloquent in his seersucker suit. So I didn't get the memo that some folks don't want to talk politics, because to disagree means you're wrong.

Cousin David is an accomplished architect, once a partner of Frank Gehry. David spent most of his career in Los Angeles and is our family's token left-wing liberal. He opined about Hillary Clinton being the "smartest person running for president," and DooDaddy listened politely.

Then we turned our attention to fried green tomatoes and green tomato jam, sweet tea and, of course, hot chicken.

Between bites, DooDaddy explained why he early voted for The Donald and why he wishes the GOP would quit pandering to the far right and let go of polarizing issues like abortion. Cousin David says DooDaddy has always been a closet liberal on civil liberties.

It's not complicated. DooDaddy is in favor of capitalism, patriotism and the government staying the hell out of our personal lives. And pass the pinto beans, please.

David, to his credit, is a wonderful listener, just like my father, perhaps because their mothers were such great talkers. Picture six sisters raised in Fayetteville, Tennessee. Might as well have been Mayberry R.F.D. Because of their shared context, DooDaddy and Cousin David have a great deal of mutual respect, despite their opposing political views. These cousins can always find common ground over fried chicken. Maybe it's a Southern thing. The only fuss is about who gets the last bite of honeybun cake.

~

Beyoncé isn't the only one who likes Red Lobster, as DooDaddy will readily attest. We hit the happening seafood spot Saturday night for some geezer-pleasin' cuisine. First off, we headed to the bar with our buzzer in hand and bellied up for cocktails. Now that my son is legal, it makes the whole grandfather/grandson bonding over booze thing a lot easier. The server promptly carded DooDaddy, which surprised and delighted him.

"Goodness, I haven't been carded in 60 years," he exclaimed, as he sipped his vodka with a splash and a twist (of lime, we clarified for the bartender).

DooDaddy was equally astonished when his grandson ordered a strawberry margarita. Being strictly old school, my father doesn't approve of "silly" drinks. No banana daiquiris or piña coladas for this geezer. If it's made in a blender or comes with an umbrella, it just ain't fittin'.

We geezer-shuffled back to our table, feeling no pain now, spry and ready to tackle some seafood. The menu at "The" Red Lobster, as DooDaddy calls it, is rather overwhelming—pages and pages of who knows what all. Luckily, our server brought a basket of cheddar biscuits right away, so we had time to peruse the plethora of choices at our leisure.

"Are your crab cakes as good as Chesapeake's crab cakes?" Doo-Daddy wanted to know. "I live in a retirement home and we have crab cakes all the time, but they're fake crab cakes," he explained to Cameron, our amiable server (who also happened to be left-handed, so we chatted about that, too). Cameron demurred, admitting he hadn't dined on Chesapeake's crab cakes, so he couldn't say for sure.

DooDaddy ended up going with a trio of things plus a cup of clam chowder and lots of cheddar biscuits and then a brownie sundae combo thing (Brownie Overboard). "There's enough food there for a platoon of hungry infantrymen," DooDaddy observed. And he wasn't wrong.

DooDaddy: "I can't get my bib over my glasses, which need cleaning by the way."

DooDaddy: "Ron asked me the other day if I wanted to sit at the 'Bad Boys Table,' and I said I don't believe I do, thank you very much." Apparently, there's a group of rowdy geezers who have way more energy at breakfast than DooDaddy does, but he gets a kick out of them. His cronies, his partners in crime, make the best of their circumstances and find humor in the little things.

DooDaddy: "I sat with Jerry at lunch the other day, and this chunky guy came over and spilled coffee on us."

DooDaddy, explaining his busy social schedule: "I'm easily talked into things."

Mac and I watched with fascination as DooDaddy tried to open a pack of saltine crackers. Picture grimaces and groans, every facial muscle engaged—it was like Samson pushing the pillars apart in the temple of the Philistines.

Then *brring ring ring* and DooDaddy answers his flip phone, because old people have to answer the phone whenever it rings, no matter what. "Oh hey, Ron. We're out at The Red Lobster having dinner. That's my story. I totally forgot about that other thing. Good to hear from you. Bye bye."

And in the end, it's not the cheddar biscuits or the fish tacos or the funny stories that matter. It's being together, fully present, in the moment and savoring it.

~

DooDaddy: "I've lost five pounds."

Me: "I thought you looked taller and thinner. Especially taller."

DooDaddy: "Why, thank you. I only had tuna salad for lunch. And macaroni and cheese, which is a vegetable. And a diet milkshake and Jell-O cake."

Me: "What makes the milkshake diet?"

DooDaddy: "The secret is two scoops of low-fat ice cream, a glass of skim milk and just an oonch of chocolate sauce. It's really good."

DooDaddy: "Do you know about Jell-O cake? They poke holes in the cake and pour the Jell-O in."

Me: "Is the Jell-O what makes it dietetic?"

DooDaddy has been gaining and losing the same five pounds for the past fifty years.

As long as I can remember, everyone in my family has watched his or her weight. When I was a teenager, I was actually too skinny and drank a gritty body-builder milkshake (decidedly not diet) every morning with my bowl of Lucky Charms in an effort to bulk up. My metabolism has slowed considerably since those halcyon days, as has DooDaddy's. He used to could skip dessert at lunch and drop five pounds in three days.

DooDaddy's only "fat" days were when he sympathetically gained 25 pounds when Gmamma was pregnant with my sister Keeling. Seems my mother craved brownies and ice cream, and my father was just keeping her company. He worked for J.C. Penney at the time and was astounded when someone referred to him as "that heavyset guy in the men's department."

DooDaddy's inner voice said, "Who, moi?" as he had always considered himself tall and thin.

"I eat like a bird," DooDaddy laments now. "Don't understand why I'm not wasting away—oh and pass the pecan pie."

Now the uber-fast Mansfield metabolism has been passed down to my pride and joy, Mac Bower, who is lean as a greyhound and shredded as an Abercrombie model. Even as a baby, he was cut— except for his precious, chubby cheeks.

Since living at The Home, and even before, DooDaddy and Gmamma have carefully written down everything they eat every day in little notebooks and then tallied up the carbs. In recent years, when I asked Gmamma what the point was of this exercise, she shrugged and said she had no idea. She was just keeping DooDaddy company. Kind of like eating brownies together while pregnant.

For reasons known only to DooDaddy, he writes his food down on a scrap of paper placemat from the dining room and then carefully transposes it to his special notebook when he gets back to the apartment. He could carry the notebook in his man bag (aka "briefcase") on his walker, but then that would deprive him of the pleasure of rewriting it later. Routines are comforting. And all that writing burns calories that can be spent on Jell-O cake and pecan pie.

~

When we were growing up, DooDaddy kept a cookie jar full of "cheap cookies"—Gmamma would buy these awful off-brand cookies that my father explained were just for when you needed to eat some cookies. No need to invest in Pepperidge Farm Milanos or even Oreos, when you were just eating to take the edge off. As he later famously exclaimed, "All cookies are good. Some are better."

But don't even get him started on brownies, which are another thing entirely.

"Everybody knows brownies are supposed to be moist and chewy, but the ones at Shannondale are dry as a bone. Just a piece of chocolate cake with a smear of icing on it, calling itself a brownie. The very idea."

That's what I love about my father. He's got standards. Cheap cookies are one thing, but you have to draw the line at faux brownies.

Chapter 5

Routines Are Comforting.
Schedules Must Be Adhered To.
Change Is Scary.

"It's the principle of the thing."

–DooDaddy

Ok, so that's really three rules in one, but they are inextricably linked. Because there are two types of geezers—those who accept their geezerness and those who don't. I have one of each. Gmamma has slowed down like an old wind-up toy rusting to a standstill. And she's ok with that. She accepts her limitations and adjusts her outlook accordingly.

Death is one thing, but change is something else altogether. Gmamma does not like change of any kind. She writes down what day it is on a scrap of paper every morning. She keeps a clock in plain view and when it's time to go to lunch or bridge or bed, it's time. You get up every morning, make your bed, get dressed and sit in your chair. You work the crossword. Therefore you exist. You're still you. And there's comfort in that.

For Gmamma, there can be no variation to these rituals. She clings to them to ground herself on Earth.

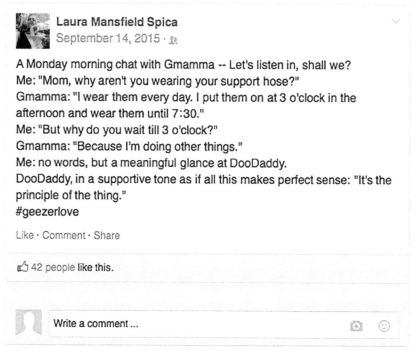

Laura Mansfield Spica
September 14, 2015 · 👥

A Monday morning chat with Gmamma -- Let's listen in, shall we?
Me: "Mom, why aren't you wearing your support hose?"
Gmamma: "I wear them every day. I put them on at 3 o'clock in the afternoon and wear them until 7:30."
Me: "But why do you wait till 3 o'clock?"
Gmamma: "Because I'm doing other things."
Me: no words, but a meaningful glance at DooDaddy.
DooDaddy, in a supportive tone as if all this makes perfect sense: "It's the principle of the thing."
#geezerlove

Like · Comment · Share

👍 42 people like this.

Write a comment ...

What I love best about my parents now is their two-peas-in-a-pod-ness. They accept and embrace each other's quirks and peculiarities. The routines they follow are like holy rituals at an Episcopal Church. Retirement leaves too much time in your day, and life at The Home revolves around the same little rituals over and over. Every day has a sameness to it. It's like the movie "Groundhog Day" in which Bill Murray's character is forced to relive the same February 2 over and over until he gains some karmic insight into his life. But for Gmamma and DooDaddy, the routines are self-imposed.

~

GEEZER UPDATE/WEEKEND EDITION: in which Gmamma gets a new pair of shoes. Friends, you will remember my ill-fated attempt to get Gmamma a new nightgown for Christmas. And you don't even want to know what DooDaddy went through trying to mail order just the right style of granny panties.

So let me tell you about Gmamma's feet (warning: graphic content). Picture, if you will, beautiful high arches and shapely ankles in spiky high heels and silk stockings. Now close your eyes and flash forward 70 years or so, add a couple of bunionectomies, hammertoes and some chronic arthritic inflammation, and you get painful, sensitive feet, like those of a retired geisha. Everything hurts. There is no relief. It's like Cinderella in reverse. It's not about fitting the right foot in the glass slipper, it's about finding the right glass slipper to fit the foot.

There's a brand called Nurture, that is soft and pliable and has an elastic strap on top—a geezer version of Mary Janes. Gmamma has one pair and has worn them to death in her thrice-daily trips to the dining room. She pads softly and shuffles in slo-mo down the carpeted halls, like Tim Conway's classic codger routine on "The Carol Burnett Show."

So Gmamma's Mary Janes are shot. And, of course, I can't find that style again. I came home with two different sizes of Merrell Shoes in a similar style. On my recent Alaskan cruise, my acupuncturist (Olga) swore by them AND there's an adjustable strap on top. I even opened a Dillard's charge account to take advantage of the 10 percent savings for the geezers.

She tried them both and dismissed them.

"I don't like change," she said, in her best Mikey-from-the-Life-cereal-commercial voice. So I returned both pairs and found a Nurture ballet flat and an ECCO Shoes Mary Jane that is the bomb. I'd wear 'em. Comfort. Style (in a hair-under-the-arms earthy kinda way).

Well, DooDaddy, former shoe department manager that he is, got down as low as he could to check the toe room … And we left her alone, no pressure, to get used to the idea of new shoes (refer to "I hate change" comment above).

I last saw her yesterday, sitting in her wingback, adorned in her orange scarf (#GBO) wearing the ECCOs, the hint of a Mona Lisa smile on her lips.

Laura Mansfield Spica
January 30, 2016 ·

GEEZER UPDATE in which we enjoy random musings from today's visit:
DooDaddy: "I wake up at 6:00 every morning and then sit down in that chair over there and wait for 7 o'clock."
Me: "What happens at 7 o'clock?"
DooDaddy: "I wake up Gmamma."
Me: "And why that chair?"
DooDaddy: "It's well situated and reasonably comfortable."
Gmamma: "I have two doughnuts and a prune for breakfast."
DooDaddy: "Then she eats one bite of her scrambled eggs and gives the rest to me. And before we can turn around, it's time for lunch."
Gmamma: "I have to eat the doughnuts, so I can take my pills."
DooDaddy: "I've been meaning to call Bob, and I've been waiting for a good time to do it, but I just haven't found one yet."
DooDaddy: "Kee called to see what Gmamma wanted for her birthday, so I told her she would like a pale gray cardigan sweater with cable stitching down the front that's not too long or too short."
Me: "And Mom wants this?"
DooDaddy: "Well, I want her to have it."
Me: "Because?"
DooDaddy: "Because I get tired of looking at her wearing the same clothes every day."
Gmamma: "And it needs to not be red or orange."
Me: "Why would it be red or orange?"
Gmamma: "Because that's what Keeling sent last time I asked for a gray sweater."
Me: "Mom, would you like to go out to lunch for your birthday?"
DooDaddy (answering for Gmamma): "That would be nice."
Gmamma (rolling her eyes): "Whatever you all want to do."
Me: "Where would you like to go?"
Gmamma (eyes finally lighting up): "Somewhere that serves sliders."
Me (surprised Mom is familiar with the term): "You mean those mini hamburgers?"
Gmamma: "Yes, I've seen them advertised on TV and I'd like to try them."
#geezerlove

Like · Comment · Share

👍 68 people like this.

 Write a comment ...

Cross your fingers (and toes) that the shoe fits and Gmamma will wear it.

Rule #5 for the Care and Feeding of Old People is threefold: Routines are comforting. Schedules must be adhered to. Change is scary.

 Laura Mansfield Spica
March 23, 2015 ·

Gmamma: "I'm getting vaguer and vaguer."
Me: "Do you still remember when to go to your hair appointment?"
Gmamma: "Yes."
Me: "And when to go to lunch?"
Gmamma: "Oh, yes."
Me: "Still working the crossword?"
Gmamma: "I work the crossword every day."
Me: "Then you're golden."
#geezerlove

Like · Comment · Share

 34 people like this.

 Write a comment ...

Chapter 6

Excursions Can Be Perilous.

D ooDaddy persists in his belief that old age is a condition that can be recovered from, like a nasty flu. Whether it's going rogue without his walker or being game for anything, including ill-conceived excursions, he's indefatigable, relentlessly optimistic, a distinguished silver Energizer Bunny. So when another resident's son, who happens to be an opera singer, was performing downtown, DooDaddy was all in.

There's a certain amount of role reversal inherent in The Care and Feeding of Old People. You become the parent, and they become the children. Demanding ones, at that. Excursions just heighten the anxiety for both parties. Remembering to put the handicapped tag on the rear-view mirror, eyeing every entry point for dangerous curbs, ever vigilant for ramps and elevators. And damn if DooDaddy isn't trying to open the door and stand up like a Jack-in-the-box before you can even get his walker out of the trunk.

It's a throwback to the days of early parenting when you juggled the baby carrier and the stroller and the diaper bag—and oops— don't forget the actual baby. There were burp cloths and sandwich bags of Cheerios, sippy cups and board books. Eldercare is oddly familiar but physically more demanding, because your geezer doesn't fit snugly in your arms.

Laura Mansfield Spica
May 5, 2015 ·

GEEZER UDATE: It's another hair-raising knee-buckling episode of the #DooDaddyChronicles in which DooDaddy takes a field trip ...
We opted to ride in the relative luxury of Joan Jetta instead of taking the #GeezerVan from Shannondale to "Mighty Musical Monday" at the historic and lovely Tennessee Theatre. DooDaddy and I were especially excited because world-renowned tenor, Mark Fox, brother of Diana Fox and son of fellow Shannondale resident, Miss Peggy (who just celebrated her 93rd birthday) was in town all the way from Aachen, Germany to perform.
The sun was shining, and all was well as we pulled onto Gay Street at 11:25 for the noon performance. Note to self: Geezers are ALWAYS early. My plan was to drop DooDaddy off out front and go park. But for some reason, the doors were not yet open and it was a logjam of walkers, wheelchairs, minivans and blue-hairs stretched for blocks. Reminded me of standing in line to see "Jaws" in 1975 at the Fox Theatre on Magnolia. I gamely stopped in the middle of the street while the light was red, hopped out, popped open the walker, got DooDaddy out and hefted him up on the curb, jumped back in the car (light no longer red) and dashed off. Felt like leaving Mac Bower at the first day of Kindergarten. He looked so vulnerable. My heart was pounding as I ran back up the hill from First Church to find my geezer still stranded on the sidewalk. Doors still locked. It was at that moment I realized we should have brought the wheelchair instead of the walker.
Finally the doors opened and the geezer stampede was on. There were box lunches to be procured (Chick-fil-A but DooDaddy couldn't eat his without mayonnaise. Too dry), popcorn to buy, that damn slanted floor I forgot all about, some goober dressed as Barney Fife scaring all the geezers, a jazz pianist lounge singer. Such a minefield of obstacles that when a well-meaning son leaned back into DooDaddy to take a snap of his sweet little momma with the faux Barney, I was ready to headbutt him.
We teetered and tottered precariously up the endless lobby, tripping on spilled popcorn, navigating around oxygen tanks, until the slant changed and we were going downhill to find a tiny velvet seat, very, very low to the ground in rows that are not walker friendly. Did I mention we should have brought the wheelchair? Finally plopped DooDaddy in a Goldilocks-sized gilded seat and dashed back for water, on account of DooDaddy was choking on his dry Chick-fil-A sandwich. Then back again for napkins. Once more for popcorn.

The Mighty Wurlitzer fired up with a "Musical Tour Across The Country" after Jack Neely spoke, and we sang Happy Birthday to a precious little cotton top. Then finally we got to the really good stuff. Let me just say Mark Fox was brilliant. Brought tears to my eyes. My heart was in my throat. Enthralling. Magical. Worth it all. The voice of an archangel, the breath control of a master yogi.

But as I listened to show tunes, spirituals and opera, over the slow purr of a nearby oxygen tank and the peaceful snoring of several geezers, all I could think about was how the hell I was gonna get DooDaddy outta there without mishap. While Mark sang, I plotted our escape ...

To Be Continued

#geezerlove

#DooDaddyChronicles

Like · Comment · Share

👍 37 people like this.

Laura Mansfield Spica
May 6, 2015 · 🔒

GEEZER UPDATE (cont.), aka "Mighty Musical Monday. The Sequel."

And so it began, the mass exodus, the slow-moving, melting glacier of white walkers making their way to the convoy of #GeezerVans parked out front.

I had hoped to bustle DooDaddy out ahead of le déluge, so I dashed to retrieve his walker where I had folded it behind the theater door, thinking I had "The Tennessee Waltz" disappearing-organ routine still to go, but they let school out early, and it was a geezer free-for-all. They were plodding but relentless in their desire to get back to their routines, now that the fun was over. I safely steered DooDaddy through the throngs down the slick-as-glass, slanting lobby floor, spilling my own popcorn in the process, frantically scanning for a chair to park him in while I went for the car. Did I mention we SHOULD HAVE BROUGHT A WHEELCHAIR?!?

Chairs are priceless in these situations. I finally appropriated one from behind a table of handouts and hefted it over my head like I'd won Wimbledon (I did not, however, kiss it). Put DooDaddy in it. Left him to wave and greet and yuk it up with everyone on the way out. He was clam-like in his happiness.

71

As I burst into the sunshine, what to my wondering eyes should appear but Ashley, the benevolent and buxom activities coordinator from Shannondale. Our #GeezerVan had prime position, and I aimed to get DooDaddy on it. That way I wouldn't have to repeat the part where I park in the middle of Gay Street and sprint, clown-like to retrieve DooDaddy and fold his walker and throw it in the trunk and him in the car, while people honk and shake their fists at me (the fist-shaking didn't really happen. People were incredibly patient and understanding. But I do hate to be a bother.)

Zigged and zagged my way back against the steady stream of humanity to tell DooDaddy the good news. Dragged him back outside to board what felt like the last chopper out of Saigon, only to find out the so-called #GeezerVan had no lift, just five very steep, corrugated metal steps. What the hell? DooDaddy pondered those rather intimidating steps for a right long while and decided he just couldn't do it. And who could blame him?

So I propped him up against the wall in the middle of the frenetic bus boardings and ran down the street to fetch Joan Jetta. Miracle of miracles a space had manifested right on the curb by the time I got back. And DooDaddy was with two friends from First Church (bless you Mert and Ashley) who helped him down the cliff-like curb to the car. And we were safely homeward bound. With only a brief stop at the Turkish tailor's shop on the way.

We arrived to find Gmamma dozing in her chair like a contented cat. She never even considered making The Incredible Journey. Why, the very idea! "Mighty Musical Monday is for the birds," she said. Sometime's Gmamma knows best.

#DooDaddyChronicles
#geezerlove

Like · Comment · Share

👍 33 people like this.

Write a comment ...

Rule #6 for the Care and Feeding of Old People: Excursions Can Be Perilous.

72

Laura Mansfield Spica
April 27, 2015 ·

And in the latest installment of what Jessica Greene has christened "The DooDaddy Chronicles," we see DooDaddy running errands, including a special trip all the way over to FM George on Central Avenue to have a key copied for $4.10, because they're the "best in town."

Next it's off to see Hussein, the Turkish tailor, who was "brought over" by John H. Daniel and when Hussein retired, he opened his own shop. Hussein is DooDaddy's tailor, and we have some trousers to be ... err, let out, due to the uncommonly good breakfasts and desserts at Shannondale.

Then we visit our favorite dermatologist, Dr. Griffith, who studies DooDaddy's face intently. He's wearing his signature goggles and miner's light, can of freezing stuff in hand, zapping various growths and spots with the zeal of a kid squirting Silly String.

I hijack DooDaddy's appointment, asking about Botox and fraxel lasers, cuz I know Dr. G. will give it to me straight. He's like the Honey Badger of dermatology. He don't care.

We cap off our morning with a late lunch at Aubrey's, because the strawberry salad is always a #geezerpleaser. We have a serendipitous encounter with Congressman Jimmy Duncan, who yuks it up and glad hands with DooDaddy. They agree something's gotta change and it's time for "the pendulum to swing" etc. etc.

Then it's back to the Old Folks Home, where I've brought Henry Dog's portrait by Kris Rehring Jones to be admired. We all agree she has captured his sweet expression perfectly.
#geezerlove

Like · Comment · Share

🖒 28 people like this.

 Write a comment ...

It's Football Time in Tennessee—the first Fall of my life without my mother, who was a two-time alumna of the university and a lifelong Volunteer football fan, having grown up in the shadow of Neyland Stadium, her childhood home where McClung Tower now stands. She was a #VFL (Vol For Life) before it was a thing.

Gmamma knew the words to all the original fight songs and was not a fan of "Rocky Top," considering it a latecomer to her treasured

Volunteer traditions. She went to football games for decades, with season tickets and a parking pass handed down from her Uncle Bob McClure, 1929 Head Football Manager. It was like a rent-controlled Manhattan apartment—until an assessment caused my parents to give up their seats. By that time, Gmamma preferred to watch the games on TV anyway. In fact, she often had to turn off the TV if she felt she was bringing her beloved Vols bad luck in any way.

For years, Gmamma dutifully donned her orange scarf and padded about the kitchen and breakfast room on Game Day (before the move to The Old Folks Home). She kept a watchful eye on the tiny rabbit-eared TV or listened to John Ward's famous play-by-play on the radio. She heated up frozen Kroger pizzas in the toaster oven for my young son, while his father and I went to the games. Mac understood that Gmamma's world didn't extend past those two rooms. He wouldn't have recognized her without her signature apron pulled up almost to her armpits over her dirndl denim skirt.

You can imagine our surprise when DooDaddy announced that he and Gmamma were going to an actual game, only a few years ago. A night game, no less, under the lights in the sweltering September heat. Because dear friends Bobby and Diana had invited them. Their premium seats were on the 50-yard line and their parking pass was "just across the street" from the stadium. Gmamma, knowing her limits, gave a sensible no thank you, but DooDaddy was never one to turn down an invitation. He still isn't.

That fateful night, Gmamma and DooDaddy (who still drove then) headed to Bobby and Diana's lakefront home for cocktails and to watch the Vol Navy from the terrace before heading to the game. Gmamma, who was prone to heatstroke, began to feel queasy but kept it to herself. If only the evening had ended then.

The merry foursome gamely carpooled through bumper-to-bumper traffic to their reserved parking spot and deftly navigated the masses of rowdy fans. Gmamma was moving in slo-mo on two artificial knees with all manner of hammertoes, bunions and tender feet that should never have left the safety of her kitchen. She was jostled and stepped on, but like a bound-foot Chinese lady, Gmamma soldiered on, nearly tumbling down the stadium steps to the choice seats. Then the digital signage lit up and the loud speakers blared "Smokey's Growl," which *Knoxville News Sentinel* columnist Sam Venable calls the "guttural attack bark" that surges through Neyland Stadium with ear-piercing frequency. It sounds like a thousand Harley Davidsons revving their engines.

The experience had changed dramatically since Gmamma and DooDaddy had last attended a game. It wasn't just the Pride of the Southland Band and Tennessee Walking Horses anymore. Navy blazers and silver flasks. It was surround sound, strobe lights and the pungent aroma of Petro's Chili & Chips. The stifling heat pulsed among the 107,000 screaming, stomping, sweating fans as they formed a never-ending human wave around the stadium.

On sensory overload, Gmamma made it until halftime.

"I'm going to be sick," she whispered to Diana, who kindly led her back up the treacherous steps and out of the stadium, assuring my mother that she, too, felt unwell. It was all too much of a muchness. DooDaddy, ever the life of the party, seemed surprised.

When I regaled my son, by then a teenager, with the fateful tale, he was nonplussed.

"Gmamma said she didn't want to go. She lives in the kitchen and the breakfast room. DooDaddy should have known better."

Karma would catch up with DooDaddy a few years later when he went to a game with my brother, hiking from the hinterlands and tailgating like an overage frat boy. The Doo could no longer go the distance.

Both geezers ultimately resigned themselves to wearing their team colors and peering over the tops of their walkers at the same little rabbit-eared TV from their Sequoyah Hills breakfast room relocated to the living room of their apartment at Shannondale.

~

When you're on the road for a #GeezerFamilyChristmas, there are some things you need to know. Once you access Delta's curbside wheelchair service that whisks your geezer past all the lines and straight down the gangplank to the plane, once you've guzzled screwdrivers in First Class (thanks to Brother Randy and his wife Sara) and tipped all the wheelchair drivers, been bustled into the crossover SUV, and arrived at your brother and sister-in-law's lovely manse, it's time to get down to business in the guest room. It's kind of like toddler proofing, except you don't really have to worry about outlet plugs.

† First thing is to remove all extraneous furniture—and by that I mean all furniture—except the bed and one sturdy chair. No side tables with knick-knacks, picture frames, paperweights, doohickies or chotchkies. These are geezer hazards and will certainly be knocked off, bumped into and broken.

† Second thing to do is to unpack all your geezer's clothes and lay them out within easy reach. If there's not a chest of drawers (geezers love drawers) just put everything on a clear surface, stacked and color coordinated. Don't forget the cloth handkerchiefs, folded just so.

† Turn down the bed like a fancy hotel. Remove all decorative throw pillows. No chocolates necessary.

† Turn on the bedside table lamp and plug in the nightlight.

† Leave the bathroom light on and clear off the sink. No scented candles, flower arrangements or potpourri. All that space will be needed for medications, Metamucil and your geezer's mouthwash of choice (for The Doo, it's a giant bottle of Cepacol, because I didn't get him any travel-sized toiletries. My bad.)

† Assemble the shower chair you shipped down ahead of time and put it in the tub where it can double as a handrail near the commode, because you may or may not be too stupid to figure out those suction-cup portable handrails (as seen on TV) that your friend lent you. Another tip I didn't follow is to buy a second walker and turn it around backwards over the commode for instant handicapped accessibility. (Again, my bad.)

† And finally, hang your geezer's favorite robe on the hook inside the closest door. Or not.

DooDaddy: "I didn't bring my robe!"

Me: silence, mouth agape, because I can't envision my father without his plaid flannel robe. This is simply not possible.

DooDaddy: "Because you weren't there to help me pack!"

Me: "But I sent Mac Bower!"

DooDaddy: "But I couldn't remember everything without you."

Me: guilty silence.

Sara and Randy have been darlings, putting the pups up, so Doo-Daddy doesn't trip over them, although one of their beloved pets had to be put down unexpectedly just after our arrival (#RIPSmokey). Don't ask. It's too sad and gruesome.

And DooDaddy keeps marveling at how narrow the doorways are—he's accustomed to The Home's generous dimensions. Trust me, there's nothing small about this house. And Sara had already rolled up the rugs to make the rooms wheelchair friendly.

So the moral of this story is; make the best of things. Be thankful for family. And love. And don't sweat the small stuff. Be in the moment. Loss looms. Grief is real. But Christmas transcends all. And family is everything.

Chapter 7

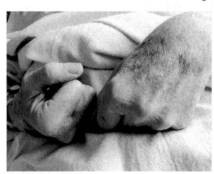

Pack A Hospital Survival Kit.

"Take a Tums and walk it off."

–Randy

Gmamma is rigidly devoted to the meal schedule at the Old Folks Home. It's as though she's a prison inmate. In fact, she is quite happily institutionalized. She lives by mealtimes. It gives her days meaning and structure. The dining room is the social hub of Shannondale. It's like the barbershop on The Andy Griffith Show. You find out all the gossip. You get to show off your family when they come to eat with you AND it's the infamous scene of the recent unpleasantness, aka, DooDaddy's broken hip.

Gmamma's version of the series of unfortunate events went something like this: "Three of us went down. Only two got up."

But there's a longer version of this particular Shannondale Shuffle. It seems DooDaddy and Gmamma had toddled into the dining room and were going to greet a new resident, welcome him to Geezertown. After all, it was the neighborly thing to do, wasn't it? The newbie has a neuromuscular disorder of some kind. DooDaddy said, "Please don't get up." But the guy wanted to stand up to speak to Gmamma, on account of his being a gentleman. That's when mayhem ensued.

Mr. Applegate sprang up like an inflatable at a used-car lot, arms akimbo, elbow braces waving in the air like ski poles on the Giant Slalom. Gmamma was taken aback. Literally. She let go of her walker and fell sideways into DooDaddy who landed on his bad hip. You know, the one with the pin in it from his near fatal car crash back in '67?

Well, I mean to tell you, canes were flying and cotton tops were falling like dominos. It all happened in slow motion like something outta "Crouching Tiger Hidden Dragon." Except instead of being set against the breathtaking landscapes of ancient China, the action unfolded over breakfast in the dining room at Shannondale. Next thing you know, DooDaddy's on morphine facing another surgery, dammit.

Because you never know when disaster will strike, you've got to be prepared.

Rule #7 for the Care and Feeding of Old People: Pack a Hospital Survival Kit.

Just as mommies-to-be have an overnight bag at the ready, children of geezers should have a hospital survival kit on standby at all times. Keep it near the fire extinguisher. When you get the call in the middle of the night, and you will—grab it and go.

I remember when I was a novice and forgot my phone charger (rookie mistake). Or blankets for the waiting room (I was the only person there without a Snuggie or a Slankit). There have been times where I've come to the ER and not left the hospital for three days. Time sort of stands still. It's like being in an airport. Or on a cruise ship.

So here are the must-have items for your Hospital Survival Kit:

† List of geezer prescriptions, insurance cards and Living Will.

† Hand lotion (because you have to keep washing your hands, and they will get dry as corn shucks, to quote DooDaddy). You need it not only for yourself but to rub on the thin-as-tissue-paper skin of your geezer, who will be bruised from IVs and all manner of needles, adhesives and rough handling.

† Reading glasses—again, bring yours and your geezer's glasses.

† DooDaddy's wristwatch. No matter when they come to, geezers want to know what time it is. The old-fashioned way. Ditto with the wedding ring. Geezers feel nekkid without it.

† Nail files and toe-nail clippers (self explanatory).

† Warm socks for geezer feet. Those hospital-issue footies aren't bad, but sometimes it's hard to get replacements when the first pair gets dirty.

† Throat lozenges. My geezers prefer sugar-free Hall's honey lemon eucalyptus. Their throats are impossibly dry from being intubated and from snoring with their mouths open.

† Books, newspapers, crossword puzzles or if you're more digital, a Kindle or iPad. Wi-Fi is notoriously poor in hospitals, but you can read what you've already downloaded.

† A notepad to scribble on fast and furiously when the doctor on rotation finally appears at 5:30 a.m. after you've been up all night helping your geezer to and from the bathroom and cleaning up the bed when you didn't make it in time.

† Chapstick—hospital air is stale and dry and see item #7 about intubation and snoring.

A flannel robe to go over the pitiful hospital gown when your geezer starts to ambulate. Dignity must be maintained at all times.

A mechanical pencil for crosswording, because a pen simply won't do (unless you're Gmamma, who insists on doing her crosswords in pen).

Those are the essentials. You can flesh out your own list as needed. And you'll want to bring Krispy Kreme Doughnuts to the nurses' station if you're around for an extended stay. These people are on the front line of eldercare. It's grueling and gross and not at all glamorous. But when it's your parent who is flailing in delirium in the middle of the night like a goldfish that flopped out of its bowl onto the linoleum, the nurses and support staff are your lifeline.

It's a best practice to know the names of all the hospital staff—technologists/technicians/transporters/hospitalists/RNs/CNAs/housekeepers/dietitions—and treat them with respect. Call them by name when you can.

Virtue is its own reward, but you'll find sweet little bonuses, like heated blankets for your geezer or unscheduled visits to let you know on the DL that the tests are in and the doctor is reviewing them now. They'll show you where the extra Styrofoam cups are stashed and help you scoot your geezer up in the bed with a little pad called, inexplicably, a "chuck."

I'm a veteran geezer wrangler now, but just a few short years ago, I was making it up as I went along. And I didn't always get the call when disaster struck. Gmamma and DooDaddy tried to hide their mishaps at first, like children ashamed of breaking a neighbor's window with an errant baseball.

Once when Gmamma was rummaging around in the basement (DooDaddy was out running errands), she fell headfirst into a box of Christmas ornaments and couldn't get out. I've fallen, and I can't get up! She was stuck for hours till DooDaddy got home and, even then, he couldn't lift her. Ended up calling the fire department to come to the rescue. As if Gmamma were a kitten stuck in a tree.

The next year she fell on the front walk on the way to the mailbox. DooDaddy usually got the mail. We still don't know why she ventured out into the wild like that. But Gmamma landed hard and broke her tailbone. She's lucky she didn't break her neck. Again, firemen were involved. And neighbors. Still, my parents hid these episodes from my siblings and me.

 Laura Mansfield Spica
January 4, 2014 ·

At the risk of becoming one of those Facebook folks who updates you on every illness and injury, I do need to report that my mother (aka Gmamma) has a broken tailbone from her fall the day after Christmas. She's lucky she landed on her bottom instead of on her head. This is the encore to last year's tumble into the Christmas ornament box in the basement. I'm beginning to think the holidays are especially hazardous ...

Like · Comment · Share

👍 7 people like this.

Write a comment ...

But when Mom refused to get out of bed one Saturday and lay curled in a fetal position, Dad did call me. My then husband and I rushed over to find her confused and mumbling.

Said her head hurt. I got her a Tylenol, which she promptly threw up. We called a neighbor who was also a retired physician. He listened to her and fretted about pneumonia.

Paramedics were summoned for what turned into a weeklong hospital stay followed by six weeks of physical therapy, occupational therapy and speech therapy. We think it was a stroke. Mom forgot my name and when I pressed her, she took a guess—Naomi?

Not even close.

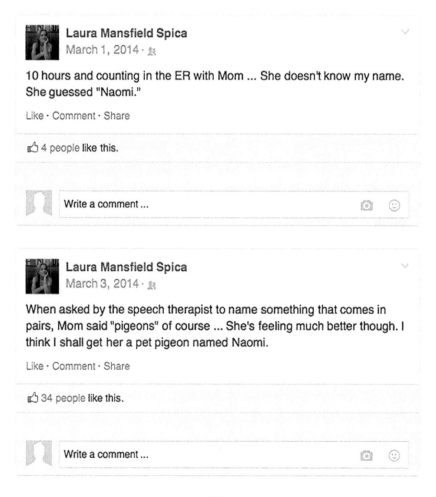

Laura Mansfield Spica
March 1, 2014 ·

10 hours and counting in the ER with Mom ... She doesn't know my name. She guessed "Naomi."

Like · Comment · Share

👍 4 people like this.

Write a comment ...

Laura Mansfield Spica
March 3, 2014 ·

When asked by the speech therapist to name something that comes in pairs, Mom said "pigeons" of course ... She's feeling much better though. I think I shall get her a pet pigeon named Naomi.

Like · Comment · Share

👍 34 people like this.

Write a comment ...

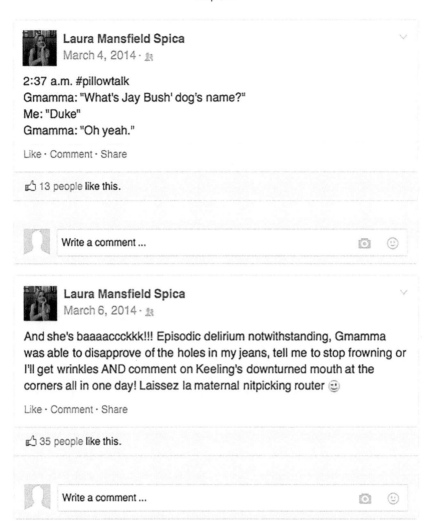

Laura Mansfield Spica
March 4, 2014 ·

2:37 a.m. #pillowtalk
Gmamma: "What's Jay Bush' dog's name?"
Me: "Duke"
Gmamma: "Oh yeah."

Like · Comment · Share

13 people like this.

Write a comment ...

Laura Mansfield Spica
March 6, 2014 ·

And she's baaaaccckkk!!! Episodic delirium notwithstanding, Gmamma was able to disapprove of the holes in my jeans, tell me to stop frowning or I'll get wrinkles AND comment on Keeling's downturned mouth at the corners all in one day! Laissez la maternal nitpicking router ☺

Like · Comment · Share

35 people like this.

Write a comment ...

~

It had been nearly impossible to get Gmamma down the steps from her bedroom to the ambulance. Some kind of chair contraption was used. That's when we knew; Gmamma and DooDaddy's days in the two-story death trap of an old brick house were numbered.

My mother swore she'd only leave feet first. But Gmamma's obstinacy and DooDaddy's acquiescence gave way after more falls down the basement steps and a T-bone car wreck turning across traffic out of the entrance to the neighborhood.

Did I mention DooDaddy's TIAs and his torn quadriceps tendon when he, too, fell on the slippery front walkway on his way to the mailbox?

My childhood home had become a house of horrors for the elderly, and still Gmamma refused to leave. So we children had a Come-To-Jesus meeting and staged an intervention. Unlike the time we rode around in synchronized panic in the carport while the Wesley House was on fire, this time we quelled our own fears and played on the fears of our parents. More on that later.

~

But first a word about watering your geezer …

I'm a firm believer in water. Always have been. Before it was chic. Tap water, room temp, no ice is my preference, but old people don't drink water. They drink coffee and iced tea, single-malt Scotch and Kentucky bourbon. Unless you count the cubes in the cocktails, there's not much H2O involved. One of DooDaddy's earliest TIAs was brought on by six cups of coffee and an afternoon of online solitaire. It started with a low-grade headache and an out-of-sorts feeling and deteriorated quickly into temporary aphasia. Once they pumped him full of fluids, DooDaddy came back to life. Like a shriveled sponge immersed in warm, soapy water, he got his color back.

Gmamma, too, is decidedly not a water drinker. It's just not a beverage to her. Something to rinse with and spit out after you brush your teeth.

The ubiquitous water bottles carried by Barre babes, soccer moms and lumbersexuals alike are just not a geezer accessory. *But*, dehydration is a huge cause of all sorts of bad things, especially neurological events. It can also cause imbalances in medicines in the bloodstream. Low sodium is a culprit. I'm just scratching the surface here, but it's the first thing to address with most health issues for geezers—check the fluid intake.

Don't even get me started on UTIs, because they are the devil.

So a best practice for the Care and Feeding of Old People is: Hydrate. Hydrate. Hydrate.

To that end, I did get Gmamma and DooDaddy matching S'well bottles for Christmas. Blue was my mother's favorite color, but I

Laura Mansfield Spica
February 6, 2016 ·

Dr. Bhandari: "Oh my, you have a large lump on your neck. When did you first notice this?"
Gmamma: "I don't know. It's been there for ages."
Me: "Mom, why didn't you say anything?"
Gmamma: "I've been pulling up my collar to hide it, so I wouldn't have to do anything about it."
#justgmamma #geezerlove

had a red one, which she spied in Joan Jetta's cupholder on an outing to some doctor's appointment or other. In typical understated Gmamma fashion, she glanced at it nonchalantly and remarked casually, "That's nice."

Seizing on the opportunity to give her something she actually wanted (Geezer readers will recall from an earlier in our story that Gmamma is like Mikey from the Life cereal commercial—she hated everything), I asked her if she wanted a S'well Bottle, too. She said she guessed that would be ok. A blue one I suggested? Nope. She wanted a red one, just like mine.

Speaking of water, it was sometimes evoked as a kind of punishment during our childhood.

"I was bugging Mom, who was reading and having her sherry in her customary silver goblet," my brother Randy recalls from his junior high school days. "I told her I was bored."

Peering at Randy over the top of her reading glasses, our mother replied evenly, "Well, you can go outside; you can read a book; you can take a nap; or you can drink a glass of water."

My brother notes that he has inherited our mother's trademark stiff upper lip and lack of sympathy for complaints of any kind. Early in his marriage to Sara, she awoke ill in the night, seeking comfort and compassion from her new husband. Randy mumbled, half asleep, "Take a Tums and walk it off."

At least he didn't tell her to drink a glass of water.

Gmamma became a grudging water drinker in the twilight of her life. Her silver sherry goblet was replaced by a red stainless steel S'well bottle, which she insisted I only fill halfway. DooDaddy is still devoted to an earlier Camelbak model in translucent blue plastic.

If you find yourself feeling addlepated or "woolly headed" (as DooDaddy would describe pre-stroke disorientation)—or if you're just bored—remember the sage advice of Gmamma and drink a glass of water.

So a best practice for The Care and Feeding of Old People is: Hydrate. Hydrate. Hydrate.

~

You can feed and water your geezers and have your emergency plan in place. Please do. It's your responsibility and your privilege. And it helps you not feel so helpless in the face of disaster and disease. The unknown. The unknowable. The monsters under the bed. But being prepared won't always keep death's demons at bay. In hindsight, I should have seen the Grim Reaper coming for my mother. But she hid all the warning signs from us. Whether she was in denial or simply accepting the inevitable, I'll never know.

But I have this to say about that. Early detection and treatment, pulling out all the stops and putting your geezer through Hell must be weighed against the alternatives. Privacy. Dignity. Quality of life. Ponder this as you sit for hours—brain numb and bone tired – by your parent's hospital bed. Listen to the beeps of the machines and watch the fluids draining in and out through tubes and bags. Feel your heart in catch in your throat with each gasp and moan from your fitfully sleeping loved one, old and frail and fragile as a newborn kitten. And whatever decision you come to, don't second-guess it after the fact. Forgive yourself and each other and keep moving forward.

Chapter 8

Pace Yourself.

"So sorry I'm late, but my mother died, you see."

Iremember the hyper-vigilant mode of early parenthood. That invisible antenna that's always scanning for signs of trouble. Of course, it never goes away. Your child is always in your heart and on your radar. For me, the parental anxiety intensified when my son started driving and again when he moved away from home. You worry about your children. But you don't worry about your parents —until they get old. And frail. And befuddled.

Then the inner monitor reactivates and re-calibrates to tune into your geezers. And it's a different kind of fear. As my son has grown up, his world has expanded, and so has my trust in him. It's the opposite with aging parents. As my parents' world gets smaller, the risks

Laura Mansfield Spica
December 3, 2015 · 🐾

Hello from the other side ...
Just a quick note to say I'm back. And thanks for all the calls and letters --
well actually, three emails & a couple of Instagram messages -- saying you
missed me and the geezers.
First of all, let me say it was a Very Geezer Thanksgiving. Nothing like last
year's festivities with four walkers and an ambulance, but festive in its own
way. I smuggled a flask into the Old Folks' Home to create the requisite
warm holiday glow. We waited in the buffet line, jostled by cotton tops, still
wearing their purses, lest they miss out on the feast. It was the geezer
version of Black Friday shopping.
Gmamma and DooDaddy are fine, although Gmamma is winding down like
a worn-out Energizer Bunny. Well, she was never the Energizer Bunny. But
picture an antique porcelain doll with pale sky blue eyes and a big key in
her back, slo-mo-ing and tilting forward in her tracks. That's Gmamma.
I think she's only staying around to ward off the rabid female fan base of
DooDaddy's, powdered and garishly lipsticked, fluttering around him like
dusty butterflies in a diorama.
"Behave," she admonished DooDaddy, as we left for her most recent
dentist appointment.
More later. I've hit a rough patch but am plodding through the puddles and
gingerly stepping around the sink holes. Hoping for smooth roads or better
treads ahead. And yes, Adele's new album is the soundtrack of my life.
Love you. XXOOO

Like · Comment · Share

👍 83 people like this.

Write a comment ...

increase and their capabilities decrease. Gmamma and DooDaddy
are more vulnerable than ever. And I am afraid for them. Always.

Although Gmamma is virtually deaf and nearly blind, she is my
father's keeper, his companion, his guardian. When he had his last
seizure, she was the one who slo-mo scrambled on her walker into
the hall of the Old Folks Home and mewed in her croaky little voice
for help. Never mind that there's a cord around her neck to pull and
a phone on the table. Her instinct was to "run" for help.

Years earlier, when my parents still lived independently, she would call me and say, "Your father is having a heart attack." Or "Your father's fallen, and they just took him away in the ambulance." When I stopped by one Saturday afternoon, Gmamma greeted me with a worried look on her face. "There's something wrong with him. He's acting funny," she whispered urgently.

DooDaddy never had a heart attack, it was a transient ischemic attack (aka TIA or mini-stroke), but my point is Gmamma had his back. And if I'm at the beach for a break from geezer care, I feel guilty as hell. What if something happens?

My son is all grown up. He's on geezer duty this week, but I'm having a hard time un-scrunching my shoulders and un-clinching my jaw. Which is exactly why I needed to get away.

A friend told me she didn't take a trip for 15 years because she was worried about something happening to her elderly mother. And then she realized that was ridiculous.

Caregivers need a break.

So I'm gonna soak up the sun and watch the water and breathe.

I'm going to try to let go of the fear that constantly grips my heart and knots my stomach. I didn't realize how bad it had gotten. Or how watching my parents suffer had affected me. Being helpless to save someone you love is the worst feeling ever.

Trusting that God holds my geezers in the palm of his hand brings me some peace. And I'm ashamed to say I had to get out of town to remember that. To focus on letting go of trying to control everything. To stop helicopter-parenting my parent.

So Rule #8 for the Care and Feeding of Old People: Pace Yourself.

I know a woman who cared for her parents for years. First her father and then her mother. And she lost herself. I didn't meet her until after her mother died.

Almost a year afterwards, in fact, and she was still floundering. Unkempt. Overweight. Apologetic.

"So sorry I'm late, but my mother died, you see," she greeted me at Starbucks. "And I just haven't been myself."

Mutual friends told me how talented and smart she was. How on and with it. I couldn't see it. She was like a before and after picture, only in reverse. She was lost.

I have another friend whose family has imploded since her father died. Siblings not speaking. Bickering over the estate. My friend cries every day. Her hair is falling out from the stress. In the year before her father died, she drove 25,000 miles and came to town 25 times to tend to his every need.

"I snapped at Abner," my friend told me with exasperation, referring to her sweet, patient husband, who loved her father as much as she did. "I wasn't mad at him, I was mad at my sisters."

Sometimes as caregivers, we lose sight of everything else in our lives. And we create a kind of unhealthy co-dependence, reversing the roles of parent and child.

Laura Mansfield Spica
June 27, 2014 ·

Took Gmamma to the doc yesterday, seeing as how DooDaddy is laid up at the hospital. Doc decided Gmamma might have a blood clot in her leg and ordered a sonogram STAT. Wouldn't let her walk anymore before the scan. Even with her walker. So we hightailed it down to Fort Sanders where they plopped her in this double wide wheelchair for ginormous people (Gmamma is not, in fact, ginormous. She is tiny and frail). So she gets admitted for the test (SPOILER ALERT: It was negative, thank you Baby Jesus).

After the scan, we hijacked the double wide like naughty schoolgirls and wheeled on up to visit DooDaddy, who was delirious. I panicked and made them do a stroke evaluation. (SPOILER ALERT: he had not had a stroke, thank you Baby Jesus). Then we had to hightail it back to Shannondale for supper (no Gmamma did not want a strawberry salad at Aubrey's instead, thank you very much). It was banana pudding night. DooDaddy would have loved it.

I have not made the bed all week, and I am wearing my husband's socks. I can't even.

Like · Comment · Share

👍 32 people like this.

Write a comment ...

And when our geezers are finally gone, we have no sense of self at all. Who were we? What were we doing before we dropped everything to care for our parents? It was only going to be temporary. It was an emergency. It was our duty.

And then weeks, months, even years later, we wake up one morning to realize our parents are dead and our health is shot and our lives are in shambles. And all we can do is watch daytime television and weep.

Don't let this happen. Just don't. Regardless of whether or not they guilt-trip you, your parents don't really want this for you. They don't want you to sacrifice everything they worked so hard for you to have. At least mine don't.

So go for a walk. Take a nap. Do something nice for yourself and try not to feel guilty about it.

Chapter 9

Manage Your Expectations. And Theirs.

That's just like you, Mommy. You're never satisfied."

–Mac Bower

I tried to convince my son to dress as DooDaddy for Halloween. All you need is a cardigan sweater and a walker to pull off the look. And reading glasses perched precariously on the tip of your nose and an honest-to-goodness cotton handkerchief in your pocket at all times. Maybe a crisply folded newspaper with the crossword puzzle halfway filled in.

DooDaddy: "What word would you use for 'nemesis'?"

Me: "How many letters?"

DooDaddy: "Oh, a whole bunch of letters ..."

Mac Bower: "Archenemy!"

DooDaddy: "That's exactly what I put!"

My son and my father are kindred spirits, you see. Mac has always had a special connection with his grandfather, whom he dubbed, "DooDaddy" long ago.

They would play with Matchbox cars when Mac was little. DooDaddy once asked where the cars were going, and my tiny son answered without hesitation, "opportunity." They were going to Opportunity.

So now, as Mac is finishing school and preparing to make his own way in the world, I hope and pray he is indeed headed to Opportunity and that he will follow in his grandfather's footsteps and work hard. DooDaddy's work ethic is legend.

And that Mac will keep reading and stay informed about the world and politics and issues, which he and DooDaddy love to discuss and debate. DooDaddy is forever curious about everything and articulate in stating his views, while respecting those that differ from his.

I hope Mac finds a lifelong companion like my parents found each other. They are like two sides of the same coin. And I want that for my son, though I've never managed to find it for myself.

Laura Mansfield Spica
March 26, 2015 ·

GEEZERHOTLINE: Gmamma has overcome her aversion to using the phone (an old school black rotary model) and has found my phone number. DooDaddy used to make all her calls for her. #ringalingaling
Gmamma: "Hello? Can you bring me a composition book, so I can write down my carbs?"
Gmamma: "Laura, it's hot in here, and I don't know how to turn down the thermostat."
DooDaddy (via his fliptop): "Laura sweetie, I need some more Cepacol mouthwash please ... and orange sections." (Not real fruit, the candied version, of course)
And on and on it goes ... like feeding baby birds.
I fly back and forth to the nest with laundry, toiletries, and various other sundries. I think about how our roles have completely reversed, and how they are so helpless and dependent. How small their worlds have become. And how protective I feel. Trying to keep them safely under my wing. Don't want them to fall out of the nest. It's a long way down. #motherbird

Like · Comment · Share

👍 39 people like this.

Write a comment ...

I pray my son chooses to see the glass as half full instead of half empty, another trait of my father's. Because happiness is a choice. And sometimes it's a difficult one.

And most of all, I hope my son remembers the bond he shares with DooDaddy and that he cultivates that same bond with his own children and grandchildren. Love. Acceptance. Accountability.

Because being a grandfather is a responsibility. And having a grandfather is a joy. Both of my grandfathers died before I was born, but I take great delight in watching my father be a grandfather to my son. The cardigan sweater and pocket handkerchief are just part of the costume. It's what's on the inside that counts.

~

My first husband and I had been married for seven years when my only son was born. I had given up hope of ever being a mother when my beautiful, beautiful, beautiful, beautiful boy arrived. Miracle baby. Indigo child. Old soul. And it was love at first sight. Like I was born to Mac's mom. I only had eyes for him. Nothing else mattered. In fact, I think his father, who already had adult children of his own and would soon become a grandfather, was a little jealous of my relationship with our son.

I kept a journal of the early days, "zombie days" as I referred to them then, and that was way before zombies were even a thing. Mac's father was Old School. He went back to work the Monday after the Friday we brought our baby home. Mac had been a wide-eyed cherub in the hospital. Good as gold, like a doll in a crèche. I cradled him in the crook of my arm, propped up in bed like a queen in my white flannel nightgown. I was wearing full mascara and sporting lush pregnancy hair (that would later fall out). Insert royal wave here.

When we got home from the hospital, the spell was broken. Mac wailed like a banshee—a tiny banshee to be sure, but a banshee none the less. The hellish homecoming was worth it. I couldn't get enough of him.

Mac was colicky and had to be held all the time. I think those early weeks of constant contact instilled in my son a great sense of security. He was always in my arms or asleep on my chest, leaving a little sticky spot from the heat of his warm baby breath. I'd wake up in a panic, forgetting I'd put him in his crib—I'd frantically clutch the empty hollow between my collarbones, fearing he'd rolled off me as I dozed.

Mac slept through the night at six weeks. Walked at nine months. Played cars and trucks with DooDaddy, taking imaginary trips to a place called "Opportunity" and going on "appointments" with his imaginary friend, Professor Williams. Mac was a delight. He was, as DooDaddy often pointed out, "the Best Boy in The World."

Gmamma offered to hire a baby nurse when what I wanted was frozen casseroles, loads of fresh laundry and TLC. She had been under general anesthesia during childbirth. Didn't remember a thing about it. She swears she spent two weeks in the hospital each time. My grandmother would drop everything and come from Knoxville to whatever small town we were living in at the time. She'd cook and clean and care for us. When Grandmother had to leave, she hired baby nurses to get up in the night when we cried, so Mom could rest. I wonder how old I was the first time my own mother actually changed my diaper?

I didn't want to miss my baby's babyhood. I wanted to savor every moment. My girlfriends who already had babies were doulas for me. Becky trimmed Mac's tiny fingernails when I was afraid I would accidentally snip off his tiny fingers. Sarah, already a mother of boys, taught me how to throw a towel down right quick while changing Mac's diaper, because the rush of fresh air made baby boys spray you in the eye like tiny garden hoses if you weren't careful.

The first year of Mac's life I spent in a happy, exhausted daze, spit-up down my back, dressed in a bathrobe. That boy could projectile vomit like an understudy from "The Exorcist."

I loved it all. His chubby little cheeks that bounced when he ran across the yard. His Teddy Bear Backpack, which I still have to this day. The way he sucked his right thumb and held a spoon in his left hand—Mac was destined to be a leftie, just like me. Without knowing it, this little guy filled all the empty places in my lonely heart and replaced my bitterness with gratitude and bliss. Being a mother made up for the hurt of not having a mother of my own.

Laura Mansfield Spica
March 30, 2015 ·

Twenty years ago today this beautiful indigo child entered the world. An old soul, he immediately ran headlong into the future and never looked back. Happy Birthday Mac Bower. I love you so. You are my reason for everything. XXOOO

Like · Comment · Share

71 people like this.

I read to Mac morning, noon and night. From board books to picture books to chapter books. From *Runaway Bunny* to *Goodnight Moon* to *Winnie-the-Pooh*. From *Tom Sawyer* to *Harry Potter* to *Gulliver's Travels*. Mac was rapt with attention, following my every word. Early on, as an exhausted single parent, I developed the ability to read aloud and let my mind wander at the same time. It became a meditation of sorts. The words were my mantra. My son's room was my sanctuary.

At bedtime, we'd recite the Lord's Prayer and the 23rd Psalm, in honor of my angel Grandmother. *Yea, though I walk through the valley of the shadow of death, I will fear no evil: for thou art with me; thy rod and thy staff they comfort me.*

Then always, from Gisela Voss's *Llama in Pajamas*, I'd say, "Goodnight my little llama."

Mac would answer "Buenas noches, mama."

So. Much. Love.

My son was and still is the apple of DooDaddy's eye. The absentee parenting of my own childhood, the stress of working long hours, the judgment, and the perfectionism have all been replaced by a doting grandfather, able to love unconditionally at last.

And Gmamma, virtually blind, deaf and usually dozing, asks about only two souls when I visit—my cat, Richard Parker, and my son, Mac Bower. While she didn't bring me casseroles or help me with laundry when Mac was an infant, she did make my son frozen cheese pizzas and watched sports with him when he was growing up. And when she still drove, she picked him up at school when he was sick and made him chicken and stars soup with saltine crackers. Being a grandmother freed my mother to show and receive affection more readily. To smile more broadly. To twinkle.

Gmamma and DooDaddy came to see Mac in Antoine de Saint-Exupéry's "The Little Prince" and Truman Capote's "A Christmas Memory," when I forced my son to do Community Theater. DooDaddy came to Mac's soccer matches, football games and swim meets long after he should have quit climbing aluminum bleachers and sitting in the broiling heat.

I always thought I wanted a little girl to love and shower with affection, to hug away the hurt of my somber inner child. When Mac was still in my belly, Mom (not yet Gmamma) made me promise to name my unborn child after her if it was a girl. Jennie Dickerson, who was named for her grandmother before her. I had been toying with Belinda or Natalie or even McKinley (Mac's name) after his paternal grandmother.

"Don't you dare name that baby 'Natalie,'" my mother roared at me, in a flash of fury. As if naming my baby anything other than Jennie would be a personal affront.

Fortunately, it was a moot point. I had a boy. Mac was Mac. And he is my reason for everything. I regret being bone tired and yelling at him as a small child. Ever articulate and self-possessed, Mac replied through his tears to one of my tirades, "Mommy, you're hurting my feelings."

He couldn't have been more than three years old.

I was working the graveyard shift at a local call center, trying to make ends meet without missing out on any Mac time. I'd put Mac to bed at 8 p.m. and get to work by 8:20. Home at 2 a.m. and then nap during the day when he napped. But I was cranky and sleep deprived.

Once when Mac was still just a wee tot strapped in his car seat, Prince's "When Doves Cry" was blaring from the car stereo as I sang along, declaring that I was just like my mother, never satisfied.

"That's just like you, Mommy," observed Mac, matter-of-factly. "You're never satisfied."

And in that instant, I vowed to not be like my mother. If I could possibly help it.

~

Mom was at her best on holidays. She sort of rose to the occasion of parenting when there was a theme to it. I remember her greeting us as we got off the school bus for Christmas break. She'd be wearing a Santa hat, and we'd haul out the boxed artificial tree and assemble it limb by limb. There was even fake fir tree-scented aerosol spray to *fzzzzzz* around the room. We'd lovingly hang our favorite ornaments and then toss a liberal amount of silver tinsel over everything, which our cat David would later vomit copiously among the presents.

We were allowed to open one gift each on Christmas Eve and then we were barred from coming downstairs on Christmas morning until the music was playing, and the tree was lit. Mom had a childlike wonder during Christmastime.

Her eyes would sparkle and her Edith Bunker voice would soar as we sang carols at church. We had Advent calendars, chocolate

Laura Mansfield Spica
December 26, 2014 ·

Soooo it was a Very Geezer Christmas!
But without the #geezerpocalypse drama of Thanksgiving.
Santa brought Depends instead of Bourbon.
Gmamma & DooDaddy were fetched by darling Daniel Malcolm Spica
instead of driving up in their stately silver Taurus,
with Gmamma swathed in pearls and fur.
We lost their stockings in the BIG MOVE from Kingston Park Drive to
Shannondale, but we made do with some surrogates from Pier One.
It took a couple of Macs to get the #geezers in and out of the house
without mishap. There was a jumble of walkers amidst the wrapping paper
debris.
But Gmamma still made me candied grapefruit peel -- it was the first and
only time she has used the stove at Shannondale. They actually had to
come plug it in for her. I would share a picture of this beloved holiday treat,
but I accidentally ate it all up.
And lo and behold, Henry Dog caught his first real live squirrel!
He was as startled as the squirrel, which was doing ninja-like somersaults
and slashing at Henry's nose with its tiny claws ... had to call Henry in
before it got ugly. Am hoping Richard Parker put the squirrel out of its
psychotic misery.
Christmas evolves. Traditions change. Squirrels get slower. So do
geezers.
But "the bell still rings for me; as it does for all who truly believe..."

Like · Comment · Share

👍 46 people like this.

Write a comment ...

Santas, eggnog, and cherished handmade decorations that would reappear every year like long-lost relatives at a family reunion. I'd go to sleep on Christmas Eve and listen for hooves on the roof, long after most kids had stopped believing in Santa Claus.

Grandmother made candied grapefruit peel at Christmas. It was an old-fashioned treat, an acquired taste really. The recipe had been handed down for generations. This was one tradition my mother continued. I dearly love the tart sugar coated leathery goodness of it. She still makes it for me every year. Even at Shannondale, where she had never even turned on the oven in her well-appointed geezer apartment. The staff plugged in the stove, and Gmamma boiled that grapefruit for days, despite her failing eyesight and her frailness. She did this out of love for me and reverence for her own mother. Carrying on this tradition is one of the ways I know that my mother does care for me, even if she doesn't always show it. She's just not demonstrative. Or overtly affectionate. But she really does love me and my siblings. I know it now.

At Easter, Mom would hide eggs indoors around the house. You know, the plastic kind with sugary artificially colored candy eggs and jelly beans inside, or maybe a wind-up Easter chick. And there was a large golden egg to be found, usually in the egg-shaped silver centerpiece on the dining room table. We'd dye hard-boiled eggs. I can still smell the vinegar if I close my eyes and inhale deeply. It's the scent of Spring. Tangy and pungent like fresh-cut grass.

Thanksgiving meant special table decorations and pilgrim candles. The good silver and china. Mom didn't really like to cook, so I took that over as a young married woman and continue it to this day. Christmas Dinner meant singleton relatives, like Aunt Edie. "This might be her last Christmas," Dad would say every year. "It's the Christian thing to do." As previously mentioned, Aunt Edie lived to be 98 years old.

Did I tell you about Aunt Edie's three-carat diamond ring and how Dad loved it? He always planned to give it to Mom. I'm not sure why it was so special to him, but jewelry took on a mystical significance for Dad. And Edie would flaunt that ring that Uncle Vic had given her, may he rest in peace. She'd say, "I don't know what

I'm going to do with this old thing …" Then she'd run down the list of step-grandchildren (she never had any children of her own) that she might leave it to just to torture Dad.

When she finally died, Aunt Edie left it to her sister, Laura, who finally died and left it to Dad, who promptly gave it to my sister Keeling, since she didn't have any "meaningful diamonds." Keeling then sold it to pay off her credit cards. Or maybe the money went toward my nephew's wedding. I'm not sure. Perhaps it was her own way of cutting the ties that bound her to Aunt Edie's judgment and criticism, posthumously, of course.

Dad was absolutely devastated by this seemingly callous gesture. Keeling only got a fraction of the ring's worth. And somehow, Dad lost his only link to the surrogate mother that Aunt Edie was for him. Vain, self-absorbed, petty, but he worshiped her. And now the family heirloom he most cherished is gone. I've only seen my father weep twice in my life. This was one of those times. It was indescribably awful.

Funny thing, Mom didn't even want the damn ring. She hated everything it stood for.

~

I am so grateful for my son's special relationship with Gmamma and DooDaddy, especially DooDaddy, who has been every bit the grandfather to Mac that his own grandfather wasn't. MacMac Maxter Baxter, the Best. Boy. In. The. World. DooDaddy came to Mac's soccer games and swim meets, his school performances and awards programs. He was there for all of it, all the things he missed out on with his own kids, because he was always working. It's the best gift my father could give me, loving my own child unconditionally.

The judgment stops with Mac Bower. My son can do no wrong in his grandfather's eyes. They are a delight to watch together. And now Mac helps care for DooDaddy with such tenderness and grace. He even "gets" Gmamma. He accepts all their geezer idiosyncrasies. Gmamma's abrupt comments, her crankiness, DooDaddy's falling asleep mid sentence. And Mac got to know his grandparents early enough to benefit from Dad's brilliant mind.

During my years as a single working mom, it was my parents who picked up Mac at Sequoyah School if he was sick, and I couldn't get there from work. They kept him when I travelled for business. When they needed a fourth for Friday Night Bridge at Second Presbyterian, they'd prop little Mac up in a chair and deal him in. Dad was part of the carpool at West High School before my son started driving. All the moms of Mac's friends *loved* my father. It was like my friend, Carleen, all over again. This was all before Gmamma and DooDaddy got really old and seriously incapacitated. Before they became full-fledged geezers.

I think my brother is sometimes jealous of the close bond my son has with our dad. "Dad called me Mac the other day on the phone," Randy will grumble. And I get that, but at the same time, oh how I wish Randy could be happy for Dad and his second chance at parenting. Even Keeling gets a bit peevish that Dad is not closer to her boys over in Memphis, his other grandsons. But I'm the only child here in town, and my son is the only grandchild close enough to bask in the awesomeness of DooDaddy. Proximity matters. And these two—Mac and DooDaddy—are kindred spirits. It makes my heart explode with happiness.

~

"How much do we owe you?" asks DooDaddy, as I deliver another batch of geezer supplies. You know, Cepacol Mouthwash, Hall's Honey Lemon Cough Suppressant Drops and BIC Retractable Ballpoint Pens (black please).

"Twenty dollars," I reply.

Then Gmamma gets out the old three-to-a-page vinyl checkbook and writes me a check, carefully noting "supplies" on the memo line.

Truth is, Depends ain't cheap, even with the downloadable coupons I receive via email. Metamucil (sugar free with orange flavor), Ocuvite, and compression stockings add up. But so what? These are the necessities of life for geezers. And these geezers are the people who paid for my braces, bought me my first car, put me through college and hosted my first wedding. They lent money to my first husband and were never repaid. They babysat for my only child, apple of my eye, and chauffeured him to and fro when I was a single working mom. In short, these are my parents. And I can never repay them for all they have done for me, financially and otherwise. So, rather than present those mile-long CVS receipts for $72.11 or $54.31, I round down to $20.

Laura Mansfield Spica
May 31, 2015 ·

These guys. XXOOO 🖤

Like · Comment · Share

👍 48 people like this.

  Write a comment ...

Twenty bucks used to be a lot of money. Remember when you got a crisp twenty-dollar bill in a birthday card as a kid, and the world was your oyster? You could go to the movies, get popcorn and still get change back from a twenty. Ahh, the good old days, when twenty dollars went a long way.

The geezers are on to me now, since they started getting deliveries from Long's Drug Store. This iconic mom-and-pop pharmacy still has a lunch counter and soda fountain serving up hand-scooped milkshakes and Ruth's house-made pimento cheese sandwiches. Long's delivers prescription medications right to your door. Recently, DooDaddy started adding toiletries and random geezer sundries to his order. Tums. Kleenex. Yellow legal pads. He has been aghast at how expensive everything is.

I still deliver geezer supplies. It makes me feel useful. I can't slow the decline in mental acuity or ease the pain of arthritic joints. I can't turn back time. But I can run errands and stock the medicine cabinet.

And on my birthday, I still get a crisp twenty-dollar bill in my card.

~

My second husband (the neuropsychologist) told me I lacked empathy for victims because of my own powerlessness to save my siblings and myself from victimization. Even my father. I can't save him from his painful childhood. But that's not how I see it. Because Dad never asked me to save him. Or pity him. He never said, "Feel sorry for me. I had it rough."

Both my parents played the cards they were dealt. And they're still playing them. Without complaint. I admire the hell outta that.

As a little girl, I used to pray to God to make me fat and make Keeling thin, because I felt certain that I could handle it and would have the discipline to lose the weight my sister struggled with. I wanted to relieve her of her suffering and save her from her pain.

And who do you think my brother called whenever his life was in tatters? When his second wife left him and cleaned out his bank accounts and their condo and went off with her old boyfriend? Me, of course, with my inherent lack of empathy. And I marveled at his courage and resilience in the face of unbearable pain.

"Why do people always want to hurt me?" he asked. It broke my heart all over again.

Perhaps I lack empathy, sympathy, and compassion for so-called "victims" who wallow in their misery, because the people my heart goes out to are the survivors. Keeling. Randy. DooDaddy. Gmamma. Mac.

I also suffer from my own version of "Survivor's Guilt." While I didn't walk unscathed from a fiery airplane crash, I did emerge relatively intact from a childhood that left deep emotional scars on my siblings. And I have risen like a singed phoenix from the ashes of two marriages that went up in flames. And I raised my own son to be fearless and intrepid and not a victim.

From an early age, Mac was taught that life is not fair.

If that makes me a bad mom, I'll own it.

Because whatever my parents did or didn't do, right or wrong, they did the best they could. And that's all any of us can do. So, no judgment. No conditional love from me. I love them unconditionally, warts and all. And I'd do anything for them. It's an honor to care for my parents in their tarnished golden years.

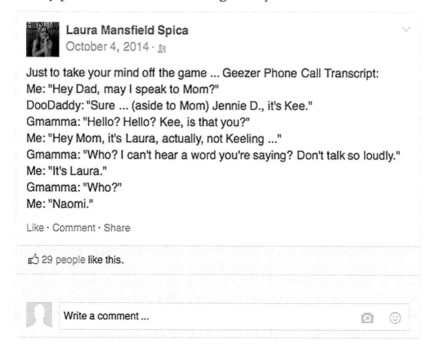

Laura Mansfield Spica
October 4, 2014 ·

Just to take your mind off the game ... Geezer Phone Call Transcript:
Me: "Hey Dad, may I speak to Mom?"
DooDaddy: "Sure ... (aside to Mom) Jennie D., it's Kee."
Gmamma: "Hello? Hello? Kee, is that you?"
Me: "Hey Mom, it's Laura, actually, not Keeling ..."
Gmamma: "Who? I can't hear a word you're saying? Don't talk so loudly."
Me: "It's Laura."
Gmamma: "Who?"
Me: "Naomi."

Like · Comment · Share

👍 29 people like this.

Write a comment ...

With the publication of *Go Set a Watchman*, Harper Lee's prequel to *To Kill A Mockingbird*, there was much hue and cry about how she depicted her father, the literary archetype of moral purity. But I don't think Atticus Finch is despicable because he has clay feet. He's human like the rest of us.

Rule #9 for the Care and Feeding of Old People: Manage your expectations. And theirs.

Chapter 10

*Growing Old Is Not For The Faint Of Heart.
Old Age Is A Full-Time Job.*

"Every day's a gift."

–GrandBud

So how does it all play out? DooDaddy and Gmamma say they want to be cremated and buried side by each in the same plot. Romantic? Meh. More like practical, since Uncle Billy famously used a family plot for his first wife, Aunt Nancy (his second wife was named Nancy, too. Or two. #creepy). This was against Grandmother's explicit instructions. She did not hold Nancy One in high regard.

Gmamma says a graveside service only. No melodramatic eulogies. Just the Lord's Prayer and "How Great Thou Art." Maybe a haunting bagpipe rendition of "Amazing Grace" in a nod to her Scots heritage. DooDaddy, on the other hand …

I once went to a funeral in Fayetteville, Dad's childhood home, to lay to rest my Great Aunt Helen. This was after Aunt Edie and Aunt Laura squabbled over the sterling silver sherbet bowls Aunt Helen had stashed under the bed and divvied up her pastel Ultrasuede suits, rationalizing that it would be wasteful to bury her in one of them.

Aunt Helen actually wrote Aunt Laura out of her will, but Aunt Laura raised such a ruckus ("I'll have what's mine"—picture Scarlett O'Hara choking on a radish and raising her fist to Heaven—"I'll never be hungry again.") that Dad and Aunt Edie split their inheritance with Laura. Bad karma, I'd say, but I digress.

When we gathered with faithful friends and family of the Kirby girls in Fayetteville, I, for one, was scandalized at the cocktail-party atmosphere that permeated the graveyard. Folks were chatting and having Old Home Week right there among the tombstones. Didn't seem fittin' to me. DooDaddy lapsed easily into his Fayetteville drawl, dropping g's off the ends of words as he greeted the ghosts of his childhood, all of whom called him "Ray-un-dee" with three syllables. The accents were so soft and thick you could have cut 'em with a butter knife.

"I'm just walkin' when I'm in Fayetteville, instead of walking," noted DooDaddy.

The service was followed by a reception at Cousin Gene's Aunt Frances Dean Barry's house. The table was laden with the requisite Southern funeral food—country ham, beaten biscuits, deviled eggs and coconut cake—bless Aunt Frances' heart.

Of course, there was congealed salad.

So, I imagine when DooDaddy passes on to his reward, we will have a receiving of friends and a memorial service so people can pay their respects and recall the glory days of Watson's on Market Square. They will reminisce about the fur (fuh) coats they bought and still wear to this day. Then the real estate folks from Dad's second career will talk about showing houses with Dad and how he could re-imagine facades and fireplaces, kitchens and family rooms for any prospective buyer. "Just knock out a wall here, and add some crown moulding there." He was the consummate salesman.

And whatever he's selling, I will always be buying, forever believing in his magical powers. Striving to please him to infinity and beyond, to eternity and back. Because pretty is as pretty does. And while I'll never be perfect in every way, I might just be ok with that. And

DooDaddy might actually love me just the way I am, despite his upbringing and his perfectionism. So we've come full circle. Hakuna Matata and all that.

If you live by the Rules for the Care and Feeding of Old People, you'll come to love and accept your geezers as flawed human beings, doing the best they can, and you'll forgive them for not getting it right. And maybe, just maybe, they will even forgive themselves.

Note: Gmamma and DooDaddy have never officially embraced the term "geezer." DooDaddy thinks of himself as more of a codger. And Gmamma, well she's not quite a dowager.

"Jennie D., how would you describe yourself?" DooDaddy asked Gmamma, when I press for clarification.

"I wouldn't," she replied.

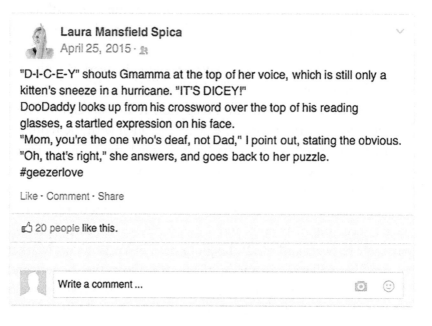

Laura Mansfield Spica
April 25, 2015 ·

"D-I-C-E-Y" shouts Gmamma at the top of her voice, which is still only a kitten's sneeze in a hurricane. "IT'S DICEY!"
DooDaddy looks up from his crossword over the top of his reading glasses, a startled expression on his face.
"Mom, you're the one who's deaf, not Dad," I point out, stating the obvious.
"Oh, that's right," she answers, and goes back to her puzzle.
#geezerlove

Like · Comment · Share

👍 20 people like this.

Write a comment ...

~

I have just been transported to the land of moonlight and magnolias, Spanish moss, gentility, and good grammar (all this to be read in your best Julia Sugarbaker voice). DooDaddy was graced with a visitation from his cousin, Gene Ham, whose grandmother, Tommie Lauderdale, was DooDaddy's grandmother Lillie Wiley's half-sister. Aunt Tommie's daughter Josephine married Gatewood Ham, the most eligible bachelor in Greenville, Miss. Lillie Wiley married Richard Kirby, born in Blount County but reared in Middle Tennessee; they later had six girls, one of whom was DooDaddy's mother Lillian. You got all that? 'Cause there might be a quiz later.

Cousin Gene is a true Son of the South, having attended Sewanee and then the University of Virginia before returning to Mississippi to live out the life of an eccentric academic. He sports a full beard on an elegantly emaciated frame that renders him anachronistic in modern clothes. He looks like a friendly spirit from another century.

I last saw him while attending my Great Aunt Helen's funeral in DooDaddy's hometown of Fayetteville, where the consonants drop off the ends of words like rose petals in the sweltering summer sun.

Although Gene grew up in Greenville, he summered in Fayetteville, after a stop in Nashville where he and his brothers, Charlie (pronounced "Chah-lee") and Billy, were outfitted in matching white linen suits right out of a Truman Capote short story. As little boys, they played together with Cousin Randy (later known as DooDaddy) among the towering seed sacks at Uncle Willy's Seed Store.

During his most recent visit, Cousin Gene was lamenting the demise of good grammar as he recounted lively anecdotes of his days as an adjunct Latin teacher at Lincoln County High School. This led to a conversation about Robert E. Lee Grammar School in Fayetteville, where DooDaddy's fifth grade teacher, Miss McKinney, wore a large diamond ring, which she had inherited. She banged it absentmindedly along the radiators as she paced the classroom. The clack clack of her diamond alerted wayward students to quit dawdling and doodling before Miss McKinney arrived to rap their knuckles with a ruler (corporal punishment was not only accepted but expected in those days).

Over white wine for courtly Cousin Gene and vodka rocks for dapper DooDaddy, the conversation meandered to so-and-so, whose husband had Parkinson's and whose mother had Alzheimer's. And blah blah blah.

Next up was a story about the "finest wing shot in the Southeast," whose potted asparagus fern became home to a daring dove. Seems she laid her eggs and hatched them right under the nose of the legendary dove hunter. His prowess was known for miles around.

"Either the dove was stupid or smart. We never knew which. But she was safe from predators under his protection," said Cousin Gene. "As he couldn't very well shoot a bird that lived on his front porch."

Gene Ham is the keeper of ancestral lore, the curator of family history and the raconteur of legends. It was he who told the woeful tale of the Cherokee mother who gifted Aunt Tommie with a deerskin beaded bag when Aunt Tommie gave her a drink of water as the shameful march along the Trail of Tears passed by the Lauderdale farm in Fayetteville.

DooDaddy hung on Cousin Gene's every word, as they swapped stories and memories and reminiscences of days gone by that were as vivid, perhaps more so, than recent events.

"Aunt Lillie was born with a foot in the road," Gene recollected, referring to DooDaddy's grandmother and her love of travel.

We bemoaned the misuse of "me, myself and I" and mourned the lost conjugation of "lie" and "lay."

I meant to stay only a few minutes but was irresistibly drawn to Gene's antiquated charm and acerbic wit. DooDaddy rose to the occasion, matching his cousin story for story. Two hours passed in the blink of an eye.

Maybe it's like this everywhere, but I suspect the genteel art of Southern conversation is rare and fragile, much like the dove in the asparagus fern.

This golden afternoon, every word was well chosen, the cadence properly paced, and the yarns spun convivially between cousins without malice or ill will.

~

So we were on vacay at Tybee Island, my second husband and I, dining at the chic shabby Sundae Cafe at Tybee. Can I just interject a YUMZ here?

Anyhow, at the next table was a befuddled old gentleman with his daughter and son-in-law. He locked his high beams on me and was instantly smitten. Yup, I got a way with the geezers, y'all. He immediately struck up a conversation with my husband, who politely but firmly shut him down. It's then that I noticed the daughter was cutting up her father's food for him.

"My dad is 79 years old. He has Alzheimer's," she explained. "Sorry to bother you. My mom's having a party, so we had to get him out of the house."

Instantly, my heart was broken, so I let him talk to me. I listened to him. Bantered with him. My husband was getting tense now. The daughter was embarrassed and asked for carryout boxes. Apparently, it's like feeding the bears. You're not supposed to do it. But how could I ignore his smiling face? His need to be acknowledged? To be seen. Heard. Understood. It's the three-fold human hunger.

The daughter bustled him out, but not before he took my hand, and we met eyes. I gave him all the warmth I could because he could be DooDaddy. And I've seen that look before in my father's eyes. Lost. Hopeful. Bewildered.

So if feeding the bears is wrong, I don't wanna be right.

~

I remember back in my twenties when my social life revolved around weddings. I think I was a bridesmaid 10 times, and there was a swirl of parties, luncheons, and rehearsal dinners leading up to each and every wedding. Then there was the actual wedding itself, the reception and the after-party. Dresses we swore we loved but never wore again. Bouquets thrown and caught. Tearful toasts and heartfelt hugs. It was a glorious time of new beginnings, fresh starts, true love and happily ever afters.

Flash forward to now, when funerals are the new weddings. Particularly for geezers, watching their gaggle of friends diminish one by one. And for the children of geezers, us sandwich-generation kids still raising our own children, these bittersweet gatherings are where we see old friends from our childhood, kiss the wrinkled faces of our parents' peers and wonder where the time has gone.

But it's not all sad. In its own way, this time is celebratory, too. We're saying goodbye to the Greatest Generation. We marvel at all they accomplished. We forgive them their shortcomings and realize we can never fill their shoes.

My dearest childhood friend recently lost her father, a contemporary of Gmamma's. And his was a life well lived. GrandBud went out on his own terms. At home. Surrounded by love. He got to say goodbye to his dog, Riley. His three daughters embraced him in a circle of devotion and adoration. He greeted friends and family who had gone on before him. They appeared as angels in his room, and he held court all night, happy to see them and ready to be reunited with his adored wife, who died a decade ago. He passed away peacefully in his sleep.

GrandBud's life motto was "Every day's a gift. Some are just harder to unwrap than others."

So we celebrated – with a Dixieland Jazz Band – the remarkable life of an exceptional man. Because funerals are the new weddings. And it's still about fresh starts and happily ever afters. About being reunited with those who've gone before. And it's glorious.

Rule #10 for The Care and Feeding of Old People: Growing Old is Not for the Faint of Heart. Old Age is a Full-Time Job.

~

DooDaddy recently told me they talked about Hospice in his discussion group at The Home.

"Isn't it boring?" one woman wanted to know. "Can I take crafts classes while I'm waiting to die?"

"It's supposed to be a medically assisted transition to the next world," DooDaddy explained, somewhat exasperated. "You're mostly asleep, with one foot through the Pearly Gates."

Because when it's your time to go, God calls you home. No crafts classes necessary.

My mother's first cousin, Nona, who was also a childhood friend of GrandBud's said, "Death is not a pretty thing. But for believers, there's nothing to fear."

And Nona is right, of course.

Chapter 11

Saying Goodbye Is Never Easy.

"Everyone's gotta go sometime."

—Gmamma

"Where's so and so?" I asked DooDaddy, over supper at the Old Folks Home (name omitted to protect the elderly). Picture a spry geezer in khakis and New Balance running shoes. He kinda reminds me of The Professor on "Gilligan's Island."

"Oh he broke the rules and got sent straight to Assisted Living," said DooDaddy, with an ominous eye roll. "He kept walking across Middlebrook Pike to the fast food places."

"Is that not allowed?" I asked, not knowing all the secret unwritten rules of Shannondale.

"Guess not," DooDaddy replied with a shrug. "That and he was falling down a lot."

So another geezer is bustled off to The Other Side. Assisted Living. Only thing worse is the actual nursing home. There are rules, you see.

Retirement facilities are businesses, after all. It's about heads in beds. And they can charge more for assisted living, so best keep your wits about you and follow the rules. It's a cautionary tale.

"Aunt Edie was oversleeping and hitting the bottle when they moved her," DooDaddy recollects. "She always did enjoy a stiff drink."

And so, as we prepared to receive the results from Gmamma's painful needling biopsies, I was wary of her options. I knew she would rather die than go to the next level of care, with or without DooDaddy.

Back when he was rehabbing from his broken hip, DooDaddy got a little complacent, letting the kindly staff at the nursing home shave and bathe him. They even opened his salt packets for him at meals. DooDaddy thought it was all just part of the service, until they threatened to keep him there, based on his inability to do anything for himself. Well, he snapped out of it right quick and started opening his own salt packets. Sugar, too. And he got to come back, returning like a war hero from The Front. Because most folks who leave in an ambulance never come back.

I remember reading an article about African villagers refusing medical help for Ebola, because to get in an ambulance was the same as death. No one ever returned to the village. It's like that in Geezerville.

Gmamma had been characteristically stoic throughout the recent unpleasantness. I'd been losing my mind, which mostly manifested in logistical mishaps like driving down one-way streets and leaving my hazard lights on after stranding Gmamma on a curb outside Fort Sanders Professional Building. I sprinted back down the sidewalk to guide my frail mother on her walker up a steep ramp in a stiff wind, her Bernie Sanders hair blowing wildly as she was buffeted about. I sat sobbing as the doctor repeatedly jabbed her in the neck to extract cell samples. She squeezed her periwinkle eyes shut tight and held onto my hands for dear life. Or maybe it was me holding onto her, because I didn't want to lose my mother. Not yet. Not like this. Her suffering was my suffering. Her pain was my pain.

After it was all over, I took her back to the apartment, where DooDaddy waited anxiously. She collapsed into her chair, exhausted and small. I offered ice packs, Tylenol, Babybel cheese, anything I could think of. But Gmamma just wanted to rest her eyes and regain her equanimity.

She grounded herself with familiar surroundings and privacy. It was like nothing has happened, and she was still in her living room back in my childhood home, surrounded by boxwood bushes, magnolias and cats.

My cousin, Rebecca, recently told me she always thought of my parents as immortal—"always there, always so very much themselves."

"When I said it, I knew the same thing I know now—it's not possible, but how I love the idea," she says. "For as long as I can remember they have been a haven of unconditional love to me and mine."

As we faced an uncertain future together, I reminded myself that this haven would always exist, beyond fear and pain, regardless of

 Laura Mansfield Spica
March 9, 2016 ·

Friends, it's been a rough week in Geezer Town.
I feel like I've lost my way.
Got lost taking Gmamma to a new doc in Farragut.
Lost my car in the Kroger parking lot with Gmamma inside it.
She was beating her tiny bird-like hands against the window
Trying to signal me, waving frantically ...
She's lost her voice so she couldn't call out to me.
I had gotten lost in the ginormous Kroger and left her in the hot car.
You're not supposed to do that with pets and babies ...
Why would I do it with my 91-year old mother?
She assured me she was quite comfortable and liked the warmth.
She has been stoic and brave. Nary a complaint while I burst into tears,
had a total meltdown and lost it in rush hour traffic.
Now I'm lost trying to connect the dots with doctors and tests
And a gruesome prognosis for my sweet momma
Who doesn't deserve any of this.
I'm at a loss. I truly am.

Like · Comment · Share

🖒 44 people like this.

 Write a comment ...

space and time. Because family is not bound by mortality. And love always wins.

~

My mother had cancer. There, I said it. I'm not going to say it again. Not going to give that C-Word power or relevance. Because words are potent, and I'd rather give power to words like Compassion. Courage. Clarity.

You'd think if you live to be 91, you've earned the right to die peacefully in your sleep. You go to bed and dream sweet dreams of paradise and pass seamlessly to the other side. No fear. No pain. Just love.

Gmamma had a pocketful of malignant tumors on her neck. We weren't sure when they appeared, because she hid them behind her Talbots mock turtlenecks, like a squirrel storing nuts for the winter. Gmamma's father, grandfather and brother were doctors. She grew up with a behind-the-mask look at medicine and a healthy respect for the horror of hospitals. To be avoided at all costs.

And then there was Gmamma's naturally stoic nature. Her high tolerance for pain. Stiff upper lip. No complaints. She was no sissy, this one.

"I've always had swollen glands," she said with a dismissive wave of her hand and a defiant lift of her chin. "Ever since I was a child."

So her tumors grew and grew until she couldn't hide them anymore. And still they kept growing. She could no longer speak above a whisper. It hurt to swallow. She was disappearing inside her new favorite cardigan sweater—pale gray, cable knit, not too short, not too long—my sister's birthday gift, as requested by DooDaddy. Only it was already too big, because Gmamma was wasting away, disappearing before our very eyes.

Biopsies would name the C-Word. Squamous cell carcinoma, Non-Hodgkin lymphoma or something equally hideous and ominous sounding. There was talk of radiation or proton therapy to keep the tumors at bay, stop them from slowly suffocating her or eating into her carotid artery or worse. Chemo and surgery were not even options due to Gmamma's frail health and congestive heart failure.

But it really didn't matter at this point. Because it was my mother's choice now. I was bound and determined to honor her wishes and swat away the well-intentioned experts and never-say-die doctors. Because this was Gmamma's life. And so it would be her death. On her terms.

Just then, when I looked into my mother's ancient face, and saw her pale blue eyes, blue as the summer sky behind her that day at the pool 50 some-odd years ago, I prayed that the Lord would hold her in the palm of his hand and give her comfort. I prayed also for my father, her partner of 59 years, that he would walk beside her on these final steps of their journey together. And let go with love when the time came.

~

Gmamma didn't even flinch when we got the news of her imminent demise.

"Everyone's gotta go sometime," she said with a shrug.

Don't mistake her casual reply for a cavalier attitude. It's just that my mother didn't fear death. She had a quiet and steadfast faith. A lifelong Presbyterian, she was at peace with her own mortality. Someone once asked her if she'd been born again, and she answered that there was no need, because she'd gotten it right the first time.

Over the week after my mother's diagnosis, we cried, my father, my siblings and I. My brother arrived from Jacksonville to say goodbye. My sister drove up from Memphis. Little did we know how soon the end would come. And how relieved we would be, despite the crushing grief.

If you have already lost your parents or are are currently caring for elderly loved ones, you understand the pain—a visceral intensity that takes your breath away and cuts your knees out from under you. But it's nothing compared to what my mother was feeling.

I had several Shirley MacLaine "Terms of Endearment" moments when Gmamma was in excruciating pain from the tumors pressing on the nerves in her neck, slowing choking her, and there was nothing I could do to help. These evil masses were only the tip of the malignant iceberg. The monster had metastasized. It lurked elsewhere in her body. We weren't sure where, because she didn't want the PET scan. So when Long's Drug Store said on a Friday it would be Wednesday before they could get her meds, I lost it right there at the candy counter.

Later as I lay crumpled on the floor at my mother's feet, my head in her lap, weeping for the loss of her and helpless to stop her suffering, she stroked my hair and told me not to cry. That everything would be ok.

Enter Wonder Woman, Mother Teresa, Xena Warrior Princess in a white lab coat—Dr. Punam Bhandari. There are no words for what this tiny, yet formidable physician did for my mother.

That final week of my mother's life was a hellish whirlwind. Denied hospice by Shannondale, she suffered in silence until Dr. Bhandari ordered palliative care. Even then, the pharmacies didn't stock the prescribed medications, so Dr. Bhandari went to Walgreens the Saturday night before Easter with her scrip pad and wrote out a prescription for whatever they had on hand. We administered droppers of liquid morphine to supplement the transdermal fentanyl patch. And still the pain persisted.

Easter morning Gmamma awoke, made her bed and padded softly out to the living room to sit in her favorite chair. She was still in her nightgown. She didn't move all day. Didn't eat. Didn't drink. Didn't speak. The monster was fierce, and we fought it with morphine. But it was like throwing a Dixie cup of water on a forest fire.

She sat all day in her favorite chair like a statue of herself.

"Where is your pain on a scale of one to ten?" my brother asked her every two hours, before administering the dropper of liquid relief. We had become the parents and she the child, obediently opening her mouth, her eyes full of trust.

She did not ask for help. Did not cry out. Just sat perfectly still with her frail, blue-veined hand on her neck, cradling the hornet's nest of tumors.

Shannondale doesn't allow hospice in the retirement community. Gmamma didn't want to go to The Other Side where wheelchair zombies roam the halls and moan all night. Her only wish was to close her eyes, lean back in her chair and die peacefully surrounded by family. I don't think that's asking too much, do you?

~

My mother did not fear death. Nor did she fear suffering. She was the strongest woman I have ever known. Her faith was abiding and steadfast. So when she and God decided it was time for her soul to take flight, take flight it did, despite what the nurses said, despite what family and friends said. Gmamma had her own timetable for departure from this earth and it was one week to the day after she told Dr. Bhandari that she did not want further tests or treatments.

Gmamma was never the last one to leave a party.

She slept deeply and awoke Monday morning, weak as a kitten. She didn't get out of bed except to go to the bathroom, because despite her opiate-induced stupor, my mother never lost her dignity.

There were tragicomic moments along the way—my sister and me dancing Gmamma from the bed to the wheelchair that my brother and I swiped from the nursing home (my brother-in-law later returned it). Me lying in bed with Gmamma, whispering that it was all right to let go, that we'd take care of DooDaddy for her, to which she replied, "I don't know what you're talking about. You people are confusing me."

Monday afternoon she became agitated and saw old friends who had long since passed on. She thought she was late for a bridge game. "Who's the fourth?" she demanded over and over again, dealing imaginary cards with a fluent motion of her hands.

A death rattle shook her chest Monday night, and then early Tuesday morning, her breath stopped. And just like that she was gone. My sister was sleeping fitfully on the sofa and noticed the sudden silence. It's hard to tell about these things, so Keeling called me just to be sure. I was already on my way over and went straight to the bedroom. There was a body there, but Gmamma had left the building. Our mother, our totem, our constant, our touchstone. Gone on from this world to the next.

I'll never forget the agonized look on my father's face when I told him the news.

Then came the haze of food and flowers—much appreciated—and the flood of faces wishing us well. I recognized the motherless among them by the look of profound empathy in their eyes. I had become a member of a special club now, no secret handshake required, just hugs and the shared experience of unspeakable loss.

Rule #11 for the Care and Feeding of Old People: Saying Goodbye is Never Easy.

I tried to do her justice in her obituary, but how do you capture a lifetime in a few paragraphs? I forgot to say she was a Girl Scout Leader and a Scotch drinker. That she loved cats, especially Richard Parker. That before she was married, she worked in advertising at Lavidge & Davis, subsisting on coffee and cigarettes. I didn't specify that memorials might be made to the Music Fund at First Church. Then again, Gmamma would have considered all these details "too much of a muchness."

The service was lovely and subdued, befitting a stoic Scots-Irish Presbyterian. As the bagpiper played "Amazing Grace" and walked slowly toward the hills, birds flew overhead. I think my mother bird was among them, wings spread, eyes on the horizon, riding the wind upward.

Days later I almost bought her raspberries at the grocery store before I remembered.

~

Working the crossword puzzle was a breakfast tradition for Gmamma and DooDaddy. In fact, it was a team sport. Gmamma did her crosswording in pen just to intimidate DooDaddy. She could pull arcane words out of the recesses of her brain. Random literary references. Whimsical quotes. Vocabulary words previously seen only on the English section of the ACT Test. DooDaddy was her wingman. He could fill in the blanks with historical figures, big band bandleaders, and song lyrics from the '40s.

Every morning, my father would make a "Xerox copy" of the crossword and put it on a clipboard, so he and my mother could simultaneously solve the clues. There was a synchronicity to their tandem wordplay, a rhythm of gentle prodding and aha moments. My parents could finish each other's thoughts and dust away the cobwebs of their collective consciousness. Over time, the process was punctuated by pregnant pauses and occasional mental blanks, the lasting effects of strokes and seizures.

It's different now. There's no reason to make a copy, but DooDaddy still does. It's part of the ritual. There's no one to help him when he gets stuck on a clue. Gmamma's candy-striped chair is empty. Still he carries on, because that's what you do, right? You get up every morning, and you go through the motions. There's comfort in the mundane. Love in the crossword puzzle clues. Magic in the memories.

So I think, when my mother grew old and frail, I tried to take care of her the way I wished she had taken care of me. I brushed her hair and painted her toenails. The little old lady she became was more accepting of my affection than the distant beautiful blonde who was my mother. Gmamma let me hug her and hold her hand, at least for a little while. And during the last two years of her life, since her stroke set off the chain of events that landed my parents in Shannondale, with matching walkers, I was closer to my mother than I ever was growing up.

Now that she is really and truly gone, I pine for my mother, the ghost of my childhood and the shadow of herself that she became, the one who let me love her.

Chapter 12

Afterward

"You can always tell a lady by her jewelry."

–DooDaddy

"I'll pick you up at 11:30, no make that 11:45," I told DooDaddy as we were making plans for Sunday Brunch at Bravo, a geezer favorite.

"Should I wear a jacket? I've got a nice seersucker one," DooDaddy asked hopefully.

"Sure, why not?" I replied, mentally upping my fashion game.

I put on a new dress (50 percent off at Banana Republic) and my mother's jewelry, because I knew it would please my father. A "dinner ring" for each hand, one in yellow gold, one in platinum, some gold bangle bracelets and the brooch/pendant made from the diamonds in my great grandmother Lida Lewis' engagement ring. Properly blinged in family jewels, I picked up DooDaddy for some brunchaliciousness.

We started off with the Doo's usual vodka rocks with a splash and a twist and my favorite peach Bellini.

Over cocktails, DooDaddy told me about his friend Willard's wife Joanie's big three-carat diamond ring and how Willard bought it for her because their son gave his wife a similar ring, and Joanie had to have one just like it.

"She wanted it, so I had to get her one," Willard told DooDaddy, who understood completely.

Jewelry carries such symbolic meaning, beyond its monetary value. Especially for my father. It has always mattered a great deal to him that my mother had nice things—"statement jewelry"—and that family heirlooms be handed down and cherished.

"You can always tell a lady by her jewelry," DooDaddy once cautioned, as if giving advice about guarding one's virginity. "Even if you fall on hard times, you must never sell your jewelry."

He also knew you buy retail and sell wholesale. Pennies on the dollar.

DooDaddy's beloved Aunt Edie, his mother figure, after his own mother died tragically of tuberculosis, had a lovely three-carat diamond engagement ring. You'll recall this tidbit from earlier in our story. Perhaps, because my father idolized Edie, her ring took on an extra magic for him. "I'll leave it to you," she promised him, and then left it to her sister Laura instead.

Edie and Laura, the two youngest (of six) Kirby girls both lived to be 98.

When Aunt Laura died, true to her word, she left the ring to Doo-Daddy, who presented it to Gmamma, like Cinderella's glass slipper.

Well, Gmamma had been judged and passively/aggressively bullied by "the Aunts" for years, and she didn't want anything to do with the legendary ring, which by now had taken on mythical status in DooDaddy's mind.

So my father gave it to my sister, who promptly sold it.

I have never seen my father so distraught. It was as if Keeling had ripped his heart out of his chest and trampled on it.

"I would have given her the money, if she didn't want the ring," he said, choking back anguished tears at my nephew's wedding. I died a little that day.

Aunt Edie's ring represented family for my orphan father. It meant acceptance and respectability and belonging for this child of the Great Depression. And my sister had inadvertently thrown all that away. Without meaning to, she had disrespected our father and everything he held dear.

Now that Gmamma has passed away, Keeling has our mother's engagement ring, a simple diamond solitaire, which DooDaddy tried to upgrade over the years, but Gmamma wouldn't consider it. It wasn't the size of the stone that mattered to her, it was the love and commitment it represented. She never removed it in 60 years of marriage. I eased it over the knuckle of her still-warm finger with dental floss the morning she died.

Just as brunch isn't really about the food, jewelry isn't really about the diamonds. It's a metaphor for family, those who are still with us, those who have left us and even those we never knew.

~

I went to visit my mother's grave the other day and was distraught that I couldn't find it. Literally. I got lost on the winding roads through the cemetery that I have driven so many times before. And when I finally found the right section, there was no trace of my mother. She died in March and on this sunshiny morning in September, there was still no engraved granite marker, no remembrance of her at all.

I have since called for a status on the stone I ordered months ago and was assured these things take time. But it was significant that I could not find my mother. I have been looking for her my whole life. Maybe like the mother bird in the classic children's book, she was off somewhere gathering food. I'm not sure. She just wasn't there during my childhood.

Mothers are supposed to be soft bundles of love. Open arms for hugs. Magnets for children, their own and others. My mother was not like that. Although she mellowed in her later years, when she morphed into Gmamma and doted on my son, she was self-contained, reserved, standoffish even. If you hugged her, you couldn't hold on too long. It's like she couldn't tolerate that level of intimacy. She was like a fluffy Persian cat that you could never pat.

I have always tried to be a different kind of mother to my son, who, incidentally, sometimes calls me "Mother Bird." I have smothered him with love and affection and acceptance. And he, like Gmamma, keeps me at arm's distance, allowing me to love him only from afar. I tell myself it's because he's all grown up. As a tiny child, he was attached to my hip, thumb in mouth, blissfully secure in our connection.

So while I miss my mother with an aching heart, I also miss the mother I never had.

~

In 1994 my first husband and I visited Montserrat, a carefree paradise known as the Emerald Isle of the Caribbean. We hiked into the Soufrière Hills Volcano that would erupt a year later, devastating the island and forever changing its topography, economy and culture. During our visit, Sam commented that Montserrat reminded him of Hawaii in the 1950s, unspoiled and lush, before it was overrun by development and tourism. That is Cuba today—a time capsule, a letter in a bottle just washing ashore.

My recent trip to Havana was a treasure chest of vibrant people, vivid colors, incredibly beautiful architecture, fragile and crumbling, yet resilient like the Cubans themselves.

My friend Liz had a special reason to visit Cuba. Her father was born and raised in Centro Habana. She wanted to find the family home he left behind in 1956 when he came to the United States to further his medical education. He subsequently married Liz's American mother. Then came La Revolución Cubana. Liz's father hasn't been home in 55 years.

We made the pilgrimage to the formerly grand, now shabby street of Padre Belascoain (formerly Padre Varela), where 86-year-old Dr. de Vega recalled roller skating on the roof and bouncing a baseball against the adjacent building. He was a city boy, so the rooftops were his playground. He and his friends flew kites with razor blades to cut the strings of other kites in the cloudless azure sky.

Liz's mother died young, and her father never remarried, raising five daughters by himself, in Oak Ridge, Tennessee, far from his boyhood home.

With the help of our gregarious taxi driver, "Johnny Walker," who had never been out of Havana, we not only found Dr. de Vega's house, we visited Santos Suarez, a suburb of Havana, where Reggie, another of our fellow travelers, was in search of his own Cuban roots. His mother and grandmother came from this now run-down neighborhood with small houses and roosters in the road. Here they practiced Santeria, the syncretic religion that grew out of the slave trade in Cuba.

Also on our trip were Nelson and Pablo, with Pablo's parents, whom Nelson affectionately referred to as "the old people." It was a multi-generational vacation for these geezers with their son and his partner, who were fiercely protective of them, despite their apparent spryness. Nelson, Pablo, his parents, Liz and I visited the famed Hotel Nacional de Cuba, situated on the Malecón in the middle of Vedado, Havana, where we sipped daiquiris and admired the view of Havana Harbor from the garden. For some reason, we decided to walk back to our hotel, the Meliá Cohiba, also located in the Vedado district.

A leisurely stroll along the sea wall, a 20-minute walk—or so we thought.

Our casual promenade soon turned into the Bataan Death March as we slogged our way back in the sweltering Cuban sun, my flimsy umbrella offering little protection. The so-called old people, Pablo, Sr. and Rosa, never complained, but Nelson was distraught, certain that his geezers were going to faint dead away from heatstroke, their last moments on this earth spent prostrate on a hot Havana sidewalk. He finally bustled them into a cab—about a block from our hotel. That's geezer love in action.

Our afternoon with the jazz dancers of the Santa Amalia Project was the highlight of the trip for me. The Santa Amalia jazz club was founded by Gilberto Torres and a group of friends who came of age dancing to Duke Ellington, Dizzy Gillespie and Cab Calloway in the '40s and '50s. The "timeless cool" of these ageless Cubans reminded me of my parents dancing through my childhood.

For Gmamma and DooDaddy, as well as for the Santa Amalia dancers, ranging in age from 75 to 95, it's all about the music and the movement, which keeps them young. My parents met on the dance floor and jitterbugged through their courtship to the same music and the same bands as these Cuban hipsters a lifetime ago in pre-Revolutionary Havana.

These charming senior citizens are young at heart, like Don Ameche and Hume Cronyn in the movie "Cocoon." Instead of a rejuvenating swimming pool, the dance floor is their fountain of youth.

Liz found her father's childhood home. Reggie communed with his Santerian grandmother. Nelson and Pablo made precious memories with Pablo's parents. And I felt my mother's presence in a jazz club in La Vibora, a far-flung neighborhood of Havana, where time stands still.

~

Remember when Wednesdays used to be Geezer Days? I'd schedule all Gmamma and DooDaddy's doctors' appointments and errands for the same day. We'd make our rounds and then eat strawberry salads at Aubrey's before heading back to The Home, where my parents would assume their positions in matching candy-striped wingbacks and doze and dawdle till dinnertime. Companionable in their silence. Or picking up the thread of a 60-year ongoing conversation.

Well, Sundays are the new Wednesdays. And there's no Gmamma. Only DooDaddy, still sitting in his striped chair, surrounded by newspapers and periodicals, stacks of junk mail and his carb-counting notebook. I sit in my mother's chair, and we visit.

Me: "Didn't you have lunch with a friend from Rotary recently?"

DooDaddy: "Let's see ... did I?"

Me: "You said somebody you used to sing with in the Rotary Glee Club came and took you out to lunch?"

DooDaddy: "Oh yes, we went to the most interesting place. I can't remember the name of it or where it was. Most exotic food. A pizza place in the middle of nowhere. Can't remember what I had, but it was very unusual."

Me: "Can we look it up in your carb-counting journal?"

DooDaddy: "Well, I don't know about that. I write my carbs down at the table, and then I put 'em in my pocket, but I don't always get 'em transcribed into the notebook."

Me: "Are you still doing your laundry ok?"

DooDaddy: "Oh yes, but you know those socks you got me that I like so well? If I wash them with anything else, they get white fuzzy balls on them, and I have to pick them off by hand if they bother me too much. It's kinda tedious. Otherwise, I just act like, 'Oh I didn't see that,' if anyone notices."

DooDaddy: "Now where is it you teach judo or whatever it is you do?"

Me: "It's yoga. Breezeway Yoga. In the breezeway at Knox Plaza by Roger's Shoe Shop and Wigs By We Three."

DooDaddy: "Oh, well I'm glad you're there, 'cause that space had been vacant for 30 years or so. You can always tell when a shopping center starts going downhill. It's all nail salons and wig shops. Stuff like that."

Me: Silence

DooDaddy to Henry Dog, who is also visiting this morning: "Henry, they just don't make dogs like you anymore, do they?"

Henry: silence

We're in a good place right now. A holding pattern, so to speak. DooDaddy's health is ok, even if his memory is slipping, and he can't quite recall what he had for lunch. But he's all up on the Syrian refugee crisis and other current events. I think about how my brief visit can't fill the empty space my mother has left behind, even though I'm perched in her chair.

We observed our first Thanksgiving without Gmamma, heading into the first Christmas of my life without her. I saw the Claxton fruitcakes at the grocery store and remembered that my mother was the only human on earth I ever knew who actually liked those. She soaked them in brandy.

I think there's a life metaphor in there somewhere among the candied cherries and nuts. About making the best of things. Because, sometimes you just have to pick the lint off your socks and get on with it.

~

A friend recently told me that her father talks a lot about not being afraid of death but being afraid of the process of dying. How well I understand those feelings, both from my parents' perspective —my beloved geezers—and my own. Because death will be a sweet release from the suffering of growing old, unwell, addled and infirm.

We're living too damn long now. Overcrowding the planet. Outlasting our friends and families and financial resources. Living longer than our bodies and minds can sustain us.

While it sounds noble in theory to cure all the illnesses in the world and find medication to treat every symptom of disease, it's just not practical. Ok, pick your jaws up off the floor. I know this sounds heartless. Or maybe I finally am becoming my mother, who was practical above all else. But her pragmatism belied a soft heart. As does mine.

A visiting pastor once remarked to the chosen frozen of First Presbyterian Church, "I don't think God's going to keep us out of Heaven for being too kind or too accepting of others." He was speaking to our tendencies to judge each other and throw religion in as the excuse. Calling something a sin instead of saying it scares us or we don't understand it. As for me, I'm a live-and-let-live kinda person. Love your neighbors. Accept people from different ethnicities, cultures and orientations, not to mention political persuasions. Let's celebrate our shared humanity.

But this business of aging affects all of us, because it puts a strain on the economy, the housing and healthcare infrastructure and the very ecosystem of our planet. I don't have any solutions or suggestions really. We should honor and revere our elderly. Keep our seniors employed longer and learn from their deep expertise and life wisdom. Create a pipeline for post-retirement reentry into the workforce. But when it comes to prolonging lives that are no lives at all, I draw the line. That's not compassion, it's cruelty. Death with dignity is the greatest gift of all for geezers.

When Gmamma's cancer first made its presence known to us, it had already been eating her from the inside out for months. And we began the whirlwind dance of desperation to diagnose and identify, to treat and cure and fix her. Pretty is as pretty does. Now all you have to do is firm up those arms. Perfect in every way. But she wasn't having it. She kept quiet until she couldn't hide her condition any longer and, by then, there was no miracle cure. My mother was ready to leave this world. And so she did. And we loved her and held her and gave her safe passage. It was a bittersweet, beautiful farewell, because she died with dignity and grace.

DooDaddy told me they have asked him to read the list of those who have passed away since last year at an upcoming event at The Home. He choked up when he told me about it, because that list includes my brave mother, his wife and soulmate.

"Can you get though it," I asked, with tears in my eyes.

"I think I can," he replied. "It's not till June, so I have time to prepare."

~

When we buried my mother, the weather didn't work for a grave-side service, so we gathered in the mausoleum instead. But the doors were open, and when the bagpiper played "Amazing Grace," she walked slowly outside, taking the music and my mother's spirit with her. My only regret from that bittersweet day was that we didn't get to greet the friends who had gathered to see her off. We were whisked back into the funeral home limo and transported to an intimate farewell luncheon. It felt somehow incomplete not to hug and thank every dear soul who sat with us. Their power of presence sustained me through that surreal morning.

Mom died after Dad's birthday and my brother's birthday but before my son's birthday. All the March men in my life. She timed it perfectly, so as not to disrupt or create a memory of sadness amidst the happiness of these celebrations. And yet, this first birthday season without her is all about her absence.

I survived the First Mother's Day. Then the First Thanksgiving. For the First Christmas, we took a well-documented Geezer Family Vacation to my brother's house in Jax. The change of scenery was a nice distraction from the usual traditions that have been forever changed by my mother's death. I have her stocking, but I didn't get it out. Didn't put up a tree. Didn't even try to make the candied grapefruit peel she made every year, like her mother before her. A special treat for me.

My first birthday without my mother was low key. Sushi with my son. My dad forgot entirely, and my sweet boy slipped away and called him, reminding him to call me and wish me well. That was in January. Then came Mom's birthday on February 9, which brought back aching waves of horror and helplessness as I relived how we discovered and then grappled with my mother's cancer this time last year, not knowing how quickly it would progress and how soon she would be gone. The hindsight unhinges me, makes my legs buckle, and I collapse with grief at her abject suffering and how I couldn't save her.

DooDaddy called the other night—March 29—to ask why my sweet cousin, Rebecca, a favorite of my mother's, had sent him yellow roses out of the blue. He was stumped.

"Don't you remember, Daddy?" I reminded him gently. "Mom died a year ago today."

And then he was crying uncontrollably, overwhelmed by his own grief at her loss and at the loss of his memory, lamenting his increasing forgetfulness and various infirmities.

A friend told me recently that he and his siblings eventually switched to commemorating their mother's birthday rather than the day she died, which seems right. A celebration rather than a somber remembrance.

My old friend Cindy, another member of the Motherless Club, explained the concept of "Yahrzeit" to me. It's a day conditioned by the need to honor one's parent in death as in life, in accordance with the Hebrew calendar. I've done that now. But I want to transition from memorials to parties.

I notice now I refer to her again as "Mom" rather than "Gmamma," as she was known in her last decades, a white fluffy grandmotherly person, soft and round, then frail and weak, clad in cardigan sweaters, flowing skirts and random scarfs. Instead, I picture her young and glamorous as she was when I was a child. And I freeze-frame her there. I wonder if that's a universal thing to do when you lose your parent or just my idiosyncratic approach. But it takes us both back to a time before sickness, loss and sadness—hers and mine. Because these last twenty-two years of my life—since I became a mother—have been marked by poignant moments of exquisite happiness but also periods of profound sorrow at dreams dashed, loves lost and marriages imploded.

And starting over. Again and again. And again.

Another friend recently told me I didn't seem like my "old self," and she was worried about me. But I've shed that skin. I'm not my old self and never can be again. It's nothing to worry about. Just the new normal. We evolve. We grow. And we are indelibly marked by life's journey, affecting us in unforeseen ways.

So as I mark this Last First, I close a chapter of my life. I officially end this season of mourning for my mother in the first year after her death. And I look ahead, hopeful and grateful, to see what's next. And I take her with me, like an angel on my shoulder and a grounding presence in my broken heart. I find that I've let go of the hurts and slights and annoyances of our complicated relationship and remember more her strength and loyalty and devotion to me and mine.

Because family was everything to my mother. And as her world got smaller and smaller, she kept us close. It's all that mattered to her at the end. That's her legacy.

Also Available From
WordCrafts Press

Past the Hood Ornament
by Mike Carmichael

A Scarlet Cord of Hope
by Sheryl Griffin

Confounding the Wise
by Dan Kulp

Morning Mist
by Barbie Loflin

What the Dog Said
by Joanne Brokaw

Pressing Forward
by April Poytner

Chronicles of a Believer
by Don McCain

www.wordcrafts.net